THE HAMMARSKJÖLD FORUMS

Case Studies

on

The Role of Law

in the

Settlement of International Disputes

The Role of Law in Population Planning

Working Paper and Proceedings of
The Sixteenth Hammarskjöld Forum

Donald H. Berman

Author of the Working Paper

Donald T. Fox

Editor

Published for

The Association of the Bar of the City of New York

by

OCEANA PUBLICATIONS, INC.

Dobbs Ferry, N.Y.

1972

Library of Congress Cataloging in Publication Data

Hammarskjöld Forum, 16th, New York, Feb. 11, 1971.
   The role of law in population planning.

   Bibliography: p.
   1. Birth control--Law and legislation. 2. Popula-
tion. I. Berman, Donald H., 1935-   II. Fox, Donald
T., 1929-   ed. III. Association of the Bar of the
City of New York. IV. Title.
Law   344.04'8   72-2061
ISBN 0-379-11816-5

Printed in the United States of America

THE SIXTEENTH HAMMARSKJÖLD FORUM

February 11, 1971

PARTICIPANTS

Donald T. Fox, presiding
Chairman, Special Committee on the Lawyer's Role in the
Search for Peace

Professor Donald H. Berman
Northeastern University School of Law;
Author of the Working Paper

Ansley J. Coale
Director, Office of Population Research,
Woodrow Wilson School of Public & International Affairs,
Princeton University; Co-Author of Population Growth and
Economic Development in Low Income Countries

Halvor Gille
Associate Director, United Nations Fund for Population
Activities;
Former Director Division of Social Affairs, United Nations
Office for Europe

Christopher Tietze, M.D.
Bio-Medical Division, The Population Council

Benjamin Viel, M.D.
Director General, Western Hemisphere Region, International
Planned Parenthood Federation; Former Director of the
Medical School, University of Chile, Author of Population
Explosion

TABLE OF CONTENTS

PART ONE

The Working Paper

A Lawyer's View of the "Population Crisis"

I.   INTRODUCTION

The provocative, bestselling author of the "Population Bomb" informs us that mass starvation is now inevitable[1] while our President warns that if present population growth rates continue for 650 years each human will have less than one square foot of turf to call his own and by the year 3520 the weight of man will exceed that of the planet.[2] We are told that this rapid increase in the world's population causes war,[3] breeds crime,[4] and threatens the destruction of our environment.[5]

Some critics of this growth pattern have urged strong anti-fertility control measures. Recently a bill was filed in the Massachusetts legislature requiring licenses to bear children; Senator Packwood has proposed limiting the number of income tax dependency exemptions available for non-adopted children;[6] and scientists suggest that involuntary fertility control will soon be required.[7]

Voices have been raised against this neo-Malthusian view of the world's expanding population. A conservative Pope,[8] new left leaders, minority group spokesmen,[9] and leaders of some emerging nations have found fertility control to be of minor importance compared to the immediate need for a massive redistribution of the world's resources.[10]

Few legal scholars have brought their analytic skills to bear on this issue even though this nation's constitutional framework providing for judicial review of most legislative and executive decisions inevitably involves the lawyer in the ultimate resolution of many basic societal decisions. Court decisions sanctioning and protecting a national bank shape monetary policy;[11] decisions involving congressional taxing powers and the breadth of the tax base affect fiscal policy;[12] litigation involving antitrust laws make lawyers the arbiters of business regulation;[13] the integration of the public schools requires that lawyers pass on education and racial policies[14]-and the list grows endlessly. Only rarely do judges deny their competence to make the broadest kind of policy decisions[15] and recently the court has further narrowed the area of judicial abstention.[16]

In reaching their decisions on these complex issues judges rely in large measure on the practicing attorney to inform them of the relevant factors necessary for an intelligent disposition of the case. When not deciding or litigating these matters the lawyer molds the society in his influential role as counsellor to the society's important institutions.

Population policy questions are fraught with thorny legal problems because so many of these issues involve fundamental constitutional rights.[17] To resolve intelligently these questions and to assist in his role of general problem solver the lawyer will have to learn some basic demographic facts, techniques, and theories.

Under a grant from the National Endowment for the Humanities I have been seeking to interrelate the lawyer's skill with the work of the demographer. This paper represents my initial observation and tentative conclusions, which briefly stated are as follows:

1. We do not have accurate figures showing the number of people who now inhabit the world.

2. Demographers have no reliable method of forecasting future population growth.

3. A conclusion that the world's population growth will begin to stabilize by the end of the century or shortly thereafter is equally as warranted as the predictions that high population growth rates will continue well into the next century.

4. Knowledge about existing or future numbers of people has limited utility because no one has formulated acceptable standards prescribing optimum population size.

5. Few facts support the widely held belief that population pressure constitutes a primary cause of societal ills but an increasing population may aggravate some problems and make them less tractable.

6. Existing population growth does not warrant the utilization of involuntary family planning methods or the wide-spread use of economic incentives in order to engender reduced fertility.

7. Most nations of the world should make voluntary family services available to their citizens and should accompany such distribution with intensive education programs stressing the desirability and methodology of population control.

II. THE NUMBERS GAME

A major industrialized nation like the United States finds it difficult to count all its citizens. In 1960 there was a well-documented substantial undercount of poor residents that inhabit the core urban areas.[18]   Much evidence now shows the undercount of the 1970 census will be even greater.[19]   However, by the use of sophisticated sampling techniques and reliance on rather accurate vital statistics we can, with reasonable accuracy, determine the number of Americans within several percentage points.[20]

Most of the world's nations take a census at regular intervals but many lack the resources to ensure an accurate count. In many of these nations one cannot rely too heavily on vital statistics because many births and deaths go unreported or the governments do not have effective centralized reporting.[21]

When western demographers attempt to measure the world's numbers they do so without any reliable figures from mainland China, a nation containing about one-quarter of the world's population.[22]   Consequently, the United Nations estimate that the world now contains 3.552[23] billion people may be off by hundreds of millions.

The method by which one seeks to forecast population growth greatly magnifies any errors existing in the initial estimate of the world's population. This method, though fairly complicated, can be briefly described.

1.   Establish a base population as of the date for which the forecast begins.

2.   Establish a schedule of vital rates that are estimated to be in effect at the date to which the base population refers -- birth, death, migration rates.

3.   Establish an estimating cycle (usually five years) and provide an estimated schedule of age-specific birth, death and migration rates that will be expected to apply during the next cycle period following the basic dates.

4.   Multiply the rate by the base population. This yields estimates of the number of births, deaths, and migrants that will occur during the next cycle period.

5.   Add (or subtract) these components to the base population, using the demographic bookkeeping equation. This yields an estimate of what the population will be at the end of the cycle. Steps 1 through 5 may be repeated for as many cycles as desired, to reach the estimated population as of some future date.[24]

Even if one could accurately establish the base population this method does not ensure accurate prognostications because the validity of the estimates rests heavily on the forecasters' capability in determining future age specific rates of mortality, fertility, and migration.

Absent some major breakthroughs in medical technology one can predict with some accuracy the future mortality rates. Except in rare situations migration had only a negligible impact on future growth.[25]   To unlock the mystery of future population growth the demographer must accurately estimate future fertility patterns and to date this key has eluded the oracle.

For example, demographers during the early part of this century warned of serious overpopulation but seriously modified their views in the 1930's and 1940's and began to speak of an impending race suicide.[26]   During this latter period a lower Ohio Court in refusing to enforce a lease provision limiting a tenancy to "adults only" stated:

"The danger of race suicide is often spoken of in these modern days, and it is not wholly an imagined danger. The power and influence of the law should be exerted in the direction of encouraging and not discouraging married couples to have offspring."[27]

Contemporary forecasters have done little better. In 1967 the U.S. Bureau of the Census projected that by the end of the century this nation would have between 283 and 361 million inhabitants.[28]   Based on the initial data from the 1970 census the Bureau has substantially lowered these estimates to between 266 million and 320 million.[29]

These predictive failures stem from the demographer's inability to foresee the volatile shifts in fertility patterns. From a high of 55 in 1800 the crude birth rate dropped to a low of 18 in the 1930's. However, from 1947-1958 the rate surged upward to 25 but by 1968 had receded to an all time low of 17.4.[30] After a period of high fertility that would have doubled our population within 70 years the country now appears to have a reproduction rate that rapidly is approaching unity. If this recent trend continues the country will experience an increase in numbers during the next few decades but the population will then stabilize by the middle of the next century.[31]

It is easy to understand why the demographer is unable to predict future fertility patterns. Demographers experience the same difficulty encountered by all forecasters of human behavior. These population forecasts are based on complex, poorly understood interrelationships among a myriad of factors which may or may not affect fertility.

For example, in failing to forecast the continuing decline in fertility that began in the United States during the late 1950's the demographer in the mid-sixties had no basis for believing that the rash of teenage marriages would subside;[32] women's liberation would become a major social force; the divorce rate would take another sharp swing upward;[33] family planning services, including abortion, would become both acceptable and available to large segments of the population;[34] or that both inflation and unemployment would soar during the last two years of the decade.[35]

Some of the predictions of substantial population increases in the United States were based, in part, on public opinion polls showing that American parents desired a family consisting of three to four children.[36] If the parents interviewed realized their goals and the subsequent generation satisfied similar desires then the 1967 predictions would have come true.

One must not place much reliance on these polls. One never knows whether the subject interviewed expresses a phantasized ideal or merely divulges his realistic desires. Many parents may desire four children but never have them because they would be unable to maintain their accustomed standard of living. To forecast properly the prognosticator would have had to foresee the downward turn in the economy and judged its impact on the fertility rate.

Secondly, polls taken in the mid-sixties cannot reflect the rapid attitudinal changes that occur in modern society. Opinion surveys showing desired high family size must be read in light of other surveys showing a more general acceptance of contraception and abortion.[37] A recent Gallup Poll showing a record low popularity for the large family might indicate that a shift in behavioral patterns is now generating an articulation of new ideals which comports with the conduct.[38]

Growth rates in many of the underdeveloped nations exceed three percent, which means their population will double within a 24 year period if such growth continues.[39] Even though many of these nations have not yet experienced a sharp decline in their birth rates there exists some basis for guarded optimism when predicting the future world population.

The rapid growth of these nations has resulted from a sharp decline in mortality.[40] Traditionally, these nations have experienced high fertility rates for two reasons: first, the high mortality rates required high fertility rates in order to maintain replacement; secondly, the agrarian family viewed male children who tilled the fields and cared for the aged parents, as a source of wealth. Since many children were female and many sons died before they could fulfill their economic function large families were deemed essential.[41]

Today these reasons for high fertility are rapidly disappearing. The introduction of basic medical and public health technology into these areas has materially lowered the mortality rate[42] and many of these nations are shifting from a rural, agrarian economy to a more technologically urban-oriented society.[43] Given less need to maintain high fertility one might anticipate a decline in birth rates.

In making its projections of 4.9 to 6.3 billion people by the year 2000 the United Nations did posit a declining birth rate even for its high estimate[44] so the only question is whether fertility will decline faster than expected. Evidence exists that this will happen.

Many nations have experienced reductions in their birth rate in excess of that predicted by the United Nations and few, if any, nations have had a reduction less than forecast. Extrapolating from these recent trends most of these nations experiencing this rapid reduction could be headed for a zero population growth within a twenty year period.[45]

More important, many of the most populous nations have embarked on vigorous family planning programs designed to educate the citizen in both the desirability and methodology of family planning.[46] Though these are experimental programs that reach only a small number of people, the results indicate that the participants, many of whom are uneducated peasants, are both willing and able to limit their families. Other nations have embarked on mammoth nationwide programs that have produced substantial reductions in fertility. Several of the heavily populated nations have embarked on nationwide programs but it is still too early to tell whether substantial reduced fertility will occur in the near future.

The United Nations prediction may have failed to forecast accurately the time within which nationwide family planning programs would be adopted and the effects of such undertakings. In addition, the future development of improved contraception, less costly abortion techniques, and methods for determining fetal sex during the early stages of pregnancy may greatly accelerate fertility reduction.

Sharp fertility declines in many underdeveloped nations cannot mask the harsh realities existing in certain nations. India, a nation one-third the area of the United States, currently has a population of 555 billion and a crude birth rate of 40-45 per 1000 per year. Even in the unlikely event that India can achieve unity in its reproduction rate by 1985, the number of Indians would swell to over one billion by the year 2040.[47] To understand the magnitude of this problem one should realize that the density of the Indian population by 2040 would be like crowding all 205 million Americans into the state of Texas. However, since both Belgium and the Netherlands handle similar densities without undue effort, even the arrival of one billion Indians need not produce disaster.[48]

I do not wish to pose as a demographer qualified to predict the future trend of the world's population. Indeed, I doubt whether demographers can successfully perform this task. However, I merely am questioning the dire predictions of human suffocation by suggesting the existence of facts that point to a less dreadful future.

Before accepting the inevitable strangulation of numbers, we might consider this passage from Norman Himes' classic work on the history of contraception first published in 1933.

"This situation, so different from the historically atypical rapid growth of the nineteenth century, has been dramatized and wept over to more than the logical limit, and has formed the basis for dire predictions and new, emotional, nationalistic appeals. I think I have shown that there are good grounds for discounting these predictions and appeals. Populations in the West are not 'doomed to die out,' and to assume that present conditions will persist is to commit a fallacy of extrapolation - into which one might reasonably expect competent statisticians not to fall. The whole history of populations adjusts to conditions more promptly than do writers on populations. The present instance is by no means the only one on record." [49]

Agreement on the number of future global inhabitants will not provide us with the standards necessary for establishing an optimum population size. For example, the world could more than double its existing population and nutritional experts assure us that feeding these numbers poses no insurmountable obstacles.[50]

Rabid nature lovers believe that the lack of untrammeled wilderness indicates that we already have too many people. It is not clear whether a majority of Americans consider the availability of wilderness as a necessary component of the good life. Furthermore, the United States has a sufficiently low population density for a major industrialized nation so that by implementing intelligent land use policies that prevented the rape of undeveloped land we could double our population and still provide the conservationist with his virgin forests.[51]

Nor can we blame the many ills of our society on population growth. To show how little population increases contribute to the deterioration of the environment Barry Commoner points out that our population since 1940 has increased about 50 per cent while mercury use has increased a hundredfold.[52] According to this ecologist our problems stem from reliance on a technology that uses mercury to produce synthetic materials for both personal and industrial consumption. Either better waste disposal methods that recaptured the mercury or continued utilization and recycling of natural materials would have avoided present high levels of mercury pollution.

Had we not abandoned pure soap for the more sophisticated detergents much of the water pollution problem might never have occurred. Furthermore, the change from the Model T to the more advanced high compression internal combustion engine has produced substantial amounts of air pollution. Granted an increased population driving more cars greater distances worsens the situation, but all these problems could be eliminated by a shift in technology that emphasized non-polluting individualized transportation, or mass transit.

Rather than blaming environmental decay on the modest increase in our numbers one could more appropriately hold our economic system accountable. Whenever the polluter utilizes the environment as a disposal area he receives a benefit for which he pays no immediate price. Failure to account for these heavy external costs encourages this destructive activity. By merely proscribing or taxing this behavior, pollution abatement will be paid for by either higher consumer prices or increased taxes.[53] To the extent that price and tax rises are anti-natalist influences the effort to curb pollution will effect a reduction in fertility.

The United States has about six per cent of the world's population and consumes vast amounts of the world's extractive resources. From these facts some advocates of population limitation argue that even slight increases of population within the United States place a great strain on the world's supply of these non-replaceable commodities.

A failure to continue to consume these resources may injure those emerging nations that sell them to the United States in exchange for the capital necessary for industrialization. Secondly, even if the United States maintained a constant population, at some point in the future a need would emerge for substitute products. An expanding population in the United States does not create the scarcity but merely hastens its arrival.

I do not quarrel with those economists who claim that high fertility rates may substantially interfere with an underdeveloped nation's attempt to augment its economic growth rate.[54] Large numbers of children increase the proportion of resources devoted to child dependency at the cost of other developmental programs. However, in determining whether to utilize coercive fertility control techniques one should recall that several nations have had rapid industrial expansion without fertility control and some nations with low fertility rates have failed to achieve substantial economic growth.[55]

Even the widely held belief that population density affects a nation's warlike tendencies will not stand up under close scrutiny. Prior to the commencement of World War II Germany feared depopulation.[56] Neither the Soviet Union nor the United States are densely populated,[57] but both have recently used their military power to suppress revolt in foreign nations. Two of the world's most densely populated nations, Britain and Japan,[58] have become increasingly pacifistic during the post-World War II period.

Nor can one attribute individual aggressive behavior to population density. In the United States most violent crime is now concentrated in the core urban areas, but many cities reporting this marked increase have had either declining or stable populations.[59] European cities have not witnessed this epidemic of violence and much of America's violent past had long runs on the less densely populated stage of the sparsely settled western frontier.

Ethnologists have noticed that increased densities lead to increased mortality rates induced by stress.[60] In urging that Homo sapiens are bound by the same laws that limit the numbers of most lower forms of animal species, Robert Ardrey noted,[61]

"Human numbers will probably never reach such magnitude as to encounter the limitations of food supply. Long before such a rendezvous can take place, other forces will have affected our numbers. If we take nature as a model there are two probabilities. The first is a sane and humane program of of population control, the second is death by stress."

From these observations Ardrey concludes,

"...As the population problem has a cultural cause, so we are provided with a cultural answer. But that answer must be mandatory. We have seen that in animal species the numbers of young are not determined by parental choice. . .we must consider enforced contraception, whether through taxation on surplus children, or through more severe means such as a conception license, replacing or supplementing the marriage license."

Unlike the animal species forming the focus of the Ardrey study, man has a proven capacity to survive for thousands of years with constantly increasing population densities while continuing to lower mortality rates.

After having studied the numbers, the means by which they were acquired and their potential significance, I have reached some tentative conclusions. There presently exist many people inhabiting this planet, and, without a major increase in the mortality rate, there are going to be many, many more by the end of the century. But no one can safely say how many more and whether the world's resources will be able to sustain the increased numbers at standards yet to be formulated.

III.   CRITERIA FOR LEGAL DECISION MAKING

One can limit population growth by only three methods -- increase mortality, increase migration or decrease fertility. A nation implementing any of these three methods can rely on the individual's desire to act in a given way; attempt to use incentives that will engender the desired behavior; or coerce the unwilling citizen.

Voluntary emigration rarely serves as a useful means of reducing overpopulation. Few crowded nations bar the exit but few citizens have both the resources and the desire to depart. Even with economic incentives the emigré may have difficulty finding a nation which will welcome him. Often those who choose to move are the most mobile citizens possessing valuable skills sorely needed by the forsaken land.

Few nations have resorted to forced emigration to solve an overpopulation problem. Such a policy compels a society to choose the group that will be forced to leave. In many situations the most logical class of emigrés would include the old and the ill -- the classes that would experience the greatest hardship by a forced move.

Throughout history one finds many cultures that lacked the medical sophistication to control population by means of contraception or abortion and deliberately increased infant mortality in order to limit their numbers.[62] Even today infanticide has advantages for the nations lacking advanced medical techniques. First, the parent need not speculate about the potentially deformed fetus. Secondly, societies that deem male children assets can control both the numbers and sex preferences. Finally, infanticide does not place an undue strain on a society that has limited medical resources.

Except for infanticide one finds few situations where society sanctions increased mortality to limit population. But unusual situations do occur when our jurisprudence seems to recognize that increased mortality may be necessary in order to allow some members of the society to survive. For example, when a crowded lifeboat begins to flounder in mid-ocean there exists legal authority that the appropriate jettisoning of some human passengers will not invoke harsh sanctions.[63]

Even the most ardent advocates of population control do not contend that existing high rates of fertility pose such an immediate threat to man's survival that a state would be justified in deliberately taking human life. Over the past years artistic elites have speculated about the eventual need or perhaps even the desirability of such action[64] but few civilized nations have adopted such a policy for population control reasons. Indeed, our society so abhors the taking of human life that few nations sanction either voluntary or involuntary euthanasia to preserve scarce medical resources.[65]

Unfortunately, society does not recognize the relatively high levels of unintended increases in the mortality rate engendered by the allocation of scarce resources. Judgment by Biafran leaders to feed the army first resulted in the death of many children. By failing to provide adequate pre-natal, maternity, and post-natal care, this nation tolerates a most uncomfortably high infant mortality rate.[66]

-11-

Dr. Benjamin Viel has noted an alarming number of unconscious infanticides throughout Latin America attributable to a parent's inability to care for large numbers of children.[67] Excess fertility may sufficiently diminish a mother's capacity to warrant a reduction in criminal charges or exoneration on grounds of insanity. However, removal of all proscriptions on this form of behavior is quite another matter.

Society could encourage such unintentional increases in mortality rates by intentionally failing to allocate resources for medical science, refusing to enforce child neglect laws or failing to provide poor families with an adequate guaranteed income. But even opponents of such welfare programs that might reduce the level of unconscious infanticide do not base their argument on a desire to limit family size; rather, they contend that society will derive greater collective benefits by adhering to a different set of priorities.

Some evidence exists that welfarism leads to reduced fertility.[68] If parents have the security that their offspring will survive to adulthood then they feel less compelled to have the "insurance" children. Moreover, the educated individual who enjoys a reasonable standard of living has greater success in limiting fertility.[69] Naturally, some fear that an unlimited family allowance program will encourage fertility. In history one finds several attempts to increase fertility through the use of economic incentives and none produced demonstrable successes.[70]

Catholics and other opponents of legalized abortion believe that this method of fertility control constitutes a conscious use of increased mortality to achieve population limitation. Lawyers can be helpful in demonstrating to the public that merely calling the fetus a "human being" sheds little light on the question of whether abortion should be legitimated.

Legal reasoning requires that we define the status of the fetus according to purposes of the law we seek to implement. For example, when death results from a mother's abandonment of a child immediately after expulsion from the abdominal cavity, the court must decide whether the fetus has become a human being for purposes of applying the homicide law.[71] If one feels that the purposes of the criminal law are furthered by such a definition then the newly born child becomes a human being.

Similarly, the desire to provide adequate compensation for injuries that might not become apparent until after birth can lead to the treatment of the fetus as a human being for certain purposes of tort law.[72] To ensure that the intent of a testator is fully realized we often give the unborn heir certain rights of inheritance shared by the living.[73]

From the early days of the common law the fetus, during the early stages of pregnancy, has not been considered a human being for the purpose of punishing either the abortionist or the parent for criminal homicide.[74]   There is fairly strong evidence that abortion during the first trimester of pregnancy only became illegal when the risks of such surgery greatly outweighed the risks of childbirth.[75]   If sound reasons exist for legalized abortion then the fetus will not be considered a human being for the purpose of protecting it from destruction, but if society desires to proscribe abortion then the fetus is granted certain protections shared by other humans.

During the late stages of pregnancy abortion begins to resemble infanticide.   Indeed, some doctors have told this author that, while performing what they believed to be a routine abortion, they have had to perform a hysterotomy resulting in the birth of a premature baby. Conversely, the performance of an abortion soon after conception does not appear to differ from the use of contraception.   In fact, some experts have argued that the IUD works by inducing an immediate abortion rather than by preventing conception.[76] If reports are accurate, medical science will soon market a "morning after" pill which works by inducing an abortion.[77]   It does not appear an unreasonable leap for a society that sanctions artificial contraception to allow abortions during the very early stages of pregnancy.

The present need to reduce fertility does not require the elimination of all restrictions on the performance of abortion. At present we have a growth rate attributable to births exceeding deaths of about .8 of one per cent.[78]   Some percentage of these pregnancies are unwanted,[79] and readily available abortion during the first trimester of pregnancy would virtually eliminate these undesired births.   There may be other reasons for allowing abortion any time prior to birth but significant limitation of population is not one of them.

To control fertility effectively by abortion, the service must be made available to all who desire it. However, the medical profession has evidently seen fit to bring great pressure to bear on government to restrict the performance of abortions to hospitals or clinics having a capacity to handle operations more complicated than a simple abortion.[80]   No doubt these restrictions will deny many women the opportunity to have an abortion.

Women's liberation and population control groups are now

mounting pressure to legalize abortion clinics staffed by paraprofessional personnel who work under medical supervision.[81] Such reform would reduce the strain on already overtaxed medical resources while ensuring that any woman who wanted an abortion could obtain one.

Reliance on abortion to limit population has numerous disadvantages. Knowledge that abortion is available may lead women to ignore less costly and safer methods of fertility control.[82] Clinical abortions performed by paraprofessionals probably will entail a greater per capita cost than most widely used contraceptive methods.

Furthermore, it should be noted that legal abortions performed by trained professionals entail some mortality and morbidity risks even though the most recent figures indicate that the complication rate in New York under the newly adopted, liberalized abortion law compares favorably with those nations which have for many years had both liberalized abortion laws and sophisticated medical technology.[83]

If the hospital abortion performed by skilled physicians results in lower mortality rates than the clinical variety, then use of this latter method may subject the less affluent patient to greater mortality risks. However, improved abortion techniques may render clinical abortions during the early months of pregnancy sufficiently safe to justify their legalization.

To my knowledge our secular law had never proscribed family planning by the use of the rhythm method or coitus interruptus. A recent court decision[84] and federal legislation[85] make clear that a full range of contraceptive services and information will be made available to all citizens who want and need them.

However, I do not believe that present growth rates have created a crisis sufficient to warrant the distribution of contraceptives that pose substantial health hazards to the user. To date, no evidence suggests that the pill presents greater mortality risk than those inherent in childbirth resulting from the failure of other forms of contraceptives.[86] Consequently, neither proscriptions on the pill's utilization nor requirements for a general warning on the pill's potential hazards are warranted.[87]

A nation seeking to reduce its fertility by reliance on voluntary family planning should ensure legalization of voluntary sterilization. Such operations, particularly for the male, are relatively safe, place few demands on scarce medical resources and have a negligible failure rate.[88] However, most sterilization procedures are designed to be irreversible. Therefore great care should be taken to ensure that those seeking the operation do so freely.

Economic incentives given to the poor in exchange for their "consent" to be sterilized would, in my opinion, amount to coercion. Advocates of rigorous fertility control have not made out a sufficient case to warrant implementation of such programs in the United States. However, sterilization programs do exist in certain underdeveloped countries and one should ask whether the crisis justifies this method of fertility control. A desire to improve economic growth does not, in my opinion, justify the imposition of such a harsh burden on the poor. However, to the extent that one can demonstrate a causal link between high fertility and increased mortality, sterilization programs may be justified.

Throughout this paper I have maintained that the prophets who foresee uncontrolled swarms of humanity have not established a case for coercive government action in the field of population control, except in those situations where the failure to limit births results in an increase in deaths. In a free society the elected leaders of the nation should be free to articulate their views on desired family size and the methods available to achieve this goal. Presumably most families are still free to disregard these admonitions and to refuse to partake in government sponsored family planning programs, if they so desire.

Constitutionally, I see no objection to sustained use of the media to convey the nation's population policy to the citizenry. Indeed, considering that about one-fifth of all brides go to the altar pregnant [89] and venereal disease has reached epidemic proportions in some areas,[90] a government might be deemed negligent in failing to so educate its people.

The public schools appear to be a most convenient place to commence this process of education and many sex education programs have a family planning component. Recently, numerous attacks have been launched against these programs. To date there is little authority to suggest that public schools cannot introduce such materials, but the validity of compulsory attendance is subject to question.

Population theorists have often maintained that numerous laws and legal institutions have an indirect effect on fertility.[91] These include laws relating to marriage, divorce, adoption, taxation, welfare, and the status of women. Before changing these laws to effect a reduction in fertility, one must consider whether any hard evidence suggests that the proposed change will produce the desired result and secondly, whether the desired effect is worth the hardship that may befall some families.

Many instances in history suggest that a rising marriage age accompanies a reduction fertility, but it is hard to prove that by

-15-

raising the marriage age one achieves a lowering of the birth-rate.[92] The present age at which people marry in this country is slowly creeping upward[93] and one might account for this increase by pointing to a number of other strongly anti-natalist factors operating in the society.[94]

With the marriage age already rising, an attempt to reduce fertility by this method would require a most significant increase in the age at which people can legally marry. Creating this legal incapacity does not comport with our other attempts to confer the rights of citizenship on the eighteen year-old.[95] Furthermore, such action might work considerable hardship in many cases involving premarital pregnancies.

Some demographers have thought that unhappily married couples unable to dissolve their union will have more children than individuals free to walk away from such a marriage and seek solace elsewhere. Logic and some statistics would support such an idea in an age where the divorced parent did not quickly remarry, or childbirth outside of wedlock was not acceptable.[96] Even though it is difficult to establish a nexus between fertility and domestic relations law, one can safely press for relaxation of our divorce laws for reasons unrelated to population limitation.

A family able to adopt children may choose to have fewer of their own. However, most families seeking to adopt are white and desire to adopt children of the same color. As the result of increased family planning services, including more readily available abortion, and less social stigma attached to raising an illegitimate child, the number of white children available for adoption has diminished.[97] Consequently, liberalized adoption laws, though desirable on other grounds, probably will have little effect on birth rates.

Several noted demographers argue that substantial reduction in fertility must await the provision of meaningful jobs for women outside the home.[98] A recently published study concludes that "an equally compelling case can be made for the reverse causal sequence; that women who have smaller families, for whatever reason, have more time to work and fewer constraints on work."[99]

But since the failure to provide the woman who seeks work with a challenging career might lead her to have more children in order to obtain a full life, those laws which ensure equal rights for women probably have an anti-natalist bias. Therefore, lawyers desiring to contribute to the reduction in fertility can begin by ensuring that their law firms do not engage in discrimination in either the hiring or promoting of women.

Logically one might conclude that the structure of the Federal income tax is a major pro-natalist influence. First, we grant unlimited tax exemptions for dependent children.[100] Secondly, the sanctioning of income splitting for spouses filing joint income tax returns provides economic incentives for marriage.[101] Thirdly, the system potentially discourages married women from working outside the home by denying day care deductions to most working mothers;[102] by failing to include the value of the housewife's services into the husband's tax base; and by utilizing the joint return so that each dollar of the working wife's income is taxed at a marginal rate equal to or in excess of the husband's.[103]

The denial of child dependency exemptions would not affect the poor who now pay no taxes, and the affluent would not find the loss of a few hundred dollars a sufficiently strong disincentive. Those most likely to respond to this kind of incentive would be the lower and middle income families who do contribute substantially to the nation's positive reproduction rate.[104]

Since ancient times governments have used economic incentives to alter fertility patterns without demonstrable success.[105] In matters as important as child rearing the taxpayers most affected by the denial of the exemptions may be very willing to pay the government several hundred dollars each year in order to have additional offspring. Of greater concern is the hardship imposed by the denial of resources to the family unit unresponsive to the penalty. Many moderate income family units will live on fewer dollars and, as a result, children will suffer from the excesses of their parents.

The need to limit population and the causal connection between modification of the tax law and reduced fertility has not been sufficiently established to override the tax policy justifications for the joint return, or the exclusion of the housewife's services from the income tax base. However, the granting of expanded child care deductions for all working mothers would not violate any established tax policy and might contribute slightly to reduced fertility.

Most systems of economic rewards or penalties directed toward the poor involve coercion, hardship or both. The denial of welfare benefits to families who have more than a prescribed number of children[106] forces innocent children to endure additional deprivation because of their elders' incontinence.

Rewards to families that practice family planning produce similar disparate treatment of children, based on the conduct of their parents. Additional payments made to a parent who undergoes sterilization cannot be viewed as consensual when made by the impoverished mother of a new-born child.

The poor of the United States who constitute only about one-fifth of the population, and whose desired family size approximates that of the affluent, do not contribute substantially to the positive reproduction rate.[107]   Until they can obtain family planning services, including abortion, we should not utilize inherently coercive incentives to influence their fertility patterns.

IV.   CONCLUSION

Evidence has not yet been adduced to warrant a finding that present or future population growth has reached crisis proportions justifying the utilization of coercive fertility control measures.   A case can be made that strong anti-natalist forces are now working to bring the United States population growth down to zero in the very near future. In many underdeveloped nations the process of demographic transition from high to low fertility has commenced and the introduction of family planning services may greatly accelerate this decline.

As attorneys, we should resist those advocates of environmental protection or economic development of emerging nations who urge a departure from our longstanding tradition of denying the government the power to determine the number of children parents may sire. In keeping with our respect for individual freedom we should remove all constraints on a person's exercising free choice by ensuring that a full panoply of family planning services, including abortion during the first trimester of pregnancy, be made available to all citizens. Such a policy complies with the declaration on population growth, human dignity and welfare signed by over 30 heads of state which provides "that the opportunity to decide the number and spacing of children is a basic human right."[108]

NOTES

1. P. Ehrlich, The Population Bomb 17 (1968).

2. Message from the President of the United States relative to Population Growth, July 21, 1969, H.R. Doc. No. 139, 91st Cong. 1st Sess. 3 (1969).

3. Ehrlich, supra note 1, at 72-80.

4. Speech of Garret Hardin delivered to American Academy For the Advancement of Science in Chicago, Ill. December 27, 1970.

5. Testimony of K. Watt, L. Day, R. Falk, G. Hardin, G. Harrar at Hearings Before the Subcommittee of the House Committee on Government Operations, 91st Cong., 1st Sess. at 9-17, 28-38, 52-56, 78, 87-89; Ehrlich, supra note 1, at 46-67.

6. S. 3632, 91st Cong. 2d. Sess.
   S. 3502, 91st Cong. 2d. Sess.

7. B. Berelson, Beyond Family Planning 38 Studies in Family Planning 1 (Feb. 1969).

8. Encyclical Letter of His Holiness Pope Paul VI on the Regulation of Birth.

9. G. Bell, Population: Scare Issue PHOENIX, May 16, 1970, p. 15.

10. At a recent conference of Southeast Asian nations, population control was not deemed a top priority item. N.Y. Times, Nov. 8, 1971, p. 9, col. 1.
    The President of Mexico in rejecting population control stated, "What I do know is that we have to populate our country...even though Mexico's death rate has fallen dramatically and its birth rate is one of the world's highest." N.Y. Times. Nov. 9, 1970, p. 26., col. 1.

11. McCulloch v. Maryland, 17 U.S. (4 Wheat.) 316 (1819).

12. When the United States Supreme Court struck down the income tax in Pollock v. Farmers' Loan & Trust Co., 157 U.S. 429 (1891) that greatly limited the government's ability to solve intelligently difficult fiscal problems. By interpreting the 16th amendment to allow Congress great latitude in establishing the tax base, the Court greatly facilitated the resolution of economic problems. See Helvering v. Brown, 309 U.S. 461 (1940); Comm'r v. Glenshaw Glass Co. 348 U.S. 426 (1955).

13. United States v. Aluminum Co. of America, 148 Fed. 416 (2d Cir. 1945): Appalachian Coals Inc. v. U.S. 288 U.S. 344 (1933); United States v. American Can 230 Fed. 859 (D. Md. 1916), appeal dismissed 256 U.S. 706 (1921).

14. Brown v. Board of Education, 347 U.S. 483 (1954).

15. Massachusetts v. Mellon 262 U.S. 447 (1923). The principle that the Court will refuse to grant a state standing to challenge, as parens patriae a federal statute was recently affirmed to the Commonwealth of Massachusetts v. Laird 91 S. Ct. 128 (1970).

16. See Baker v. Carr 369 U.S. 186 (1962); Flast v. Cohen 396 U.S. 83 (1968).

17. For example, in Griswold v. Connecticut, 381 U.S. 479 (1965) the Court fashioned a constitutional right to privacy in the marital relationship in order to strike down a state statute proscribing the use of artificial contraceptives. The California court in People v. Belous 71 Cal. 2d 954, 80 Cal. Rptr. 359, 458 P. 2d 194 (1969), cert. den. 397 U.S. 920, struck down its state abortion law on constitutional grounds.

18. J. Siegel, Completeness of Coverage of the Nonwhite Population in the 1960 Census and Current Estimate and Some Implications, in SOCIAL STATISTICS AND THE CITY 13 (Heer ed. 1956); L. Pritzker and N. Rothwell, Procedural Difficulties in Taking Past Censuses in Predominantly Negro, Puerto Rican, and Mexican Areas, id. at 55.

19. See N.Y. Times, July 23, 1971, p. 28, col. 1.

20. See J. Siegel, supra note 18.

21. United Nations, Demographic Year Book 1969, 10-11 (1970).

22. Id. at 2.

23. Id. at 115.

24. Bogue, Principles of Demography   876-77 (1969).

25. One notable exception is the United States. Since 1790 the population of the United States had doubled five times by 1950 and the 45 million immigrants who came from Europe contributed substantially to this growth. Hauser, The Population of the United States, Retrospect and Prospects,THE POPULATION DILEMMA 85 (Hauser ed. 1969).

26. Hutchinson,   The Population Debate   1-2   (1967).

27. Lamont Bldg. Co. v. Court, 66 N.E. 2d 552 (Ohio App. 1946). rev'd 187 Ohio 183. The reversal was not based on the lower judge's prediction of future population but rather on the relevance of this prediction to the determination of property rights.

28. Hauser, supra note 25, at 89-90.

29. N.Y. Times, August 13, 1971, p. 66., col. 2.

30. Hauser, supra note 25, at 86.

31. Speech of Dr. Taeuber, Associate Director of Census Bureau reported in the N.Y. Times, Jan. 14, 1971, p. 1., col. 5.

32. The 1970 Census shows a lower percentage of married persons in every age group from 16 to 24 today than 10 years ago. In 1960 59.7% of all 19 year old women were single, but by 1968 this figure had climbed to 70.4%. N.Y. Times, Jan. 31, 1971, p. 56., col. 3.

33. The divorce rate increased by one-third during the past decade. N.Y. Times, Feb. 1, 1971, p. 32, col. 1.

34. A 1969 poll revealed that 63% of Catholic women opposed Papal Encyclical proscribing artificial contraception and that 64% of those women had used non-approved methods. Westoff and Ryder, United States: The Papal Encyclical and Catholic Practice and Attitudes, 1969, 50 STUDIES IN FAMILY PLANNING, (Publication of the Population Council, 1970). A recent poll of Massachusetts residents who live in a state with restrictive laws governing distribution of contraceptives to single persons and abortion revealed that 69% favored liberalized distribution of contraceptives and 62% favored abortion with consent of both woman and doctor. Boston Globe, March 24, 1971, p. 5, col. 1.

35. The consumer price index has increased from a 1949 level of 83 to an October 1970 level of 137.4. Monthly Labor Review, Dec. 1970, pp. 81-2. During the peak of the post war baby boom, unemployment rates remained relatively low except for the years 1949 and 1950. However, from the late fifties through the middle sixties, high unemployment rates prevailed and a noticeable decline in the birth rate became apparent. Monthly Labor Review, Dec. 1970, p. 65. One should not, however, conclude a direct correlation exists between these economic indicators and fertility patterns.

36. J. Blake, Ideal Family Size Among White Americans. A Quarter of a Century's Evidence. 3 DEMOGRAPHY 154 (1966).

37. See note 34, supra.

38. N.Y. Times, Feb. 21, 1971. p. 31, col. 1.

39. Bogue, supra note 24, at 869.

40. Id. at 74-77.

41. 26 Population Bulletin 7 (Nov. 1970).

42. United Nations, World Population Prospects 45-46 (1966).

43. Bogue, supra note 24, at 469.

44. United Nations, supra note 42, at 3-4.

45. Bogue, supra note 24, at 881-83. The United Nations does not take such a sanguine view even though the experts have noted a general, world-wide decline in fertility. United Nations, Demographic Year Book 1969 1 (1970).

46. For a good summary of "The World Movement Toward Fertility Control" see Bogue, supra note 24, at Ch. 20.

47. 26 Population Bulletin No. 5, at 2 (1970).

48. Belgium and the Netherlands, respectively, have 316 and 315 persons per square kilometer. United Nations, supra note 21, at 120.

49. N. Himes, Medical History of Contraception 417 (Schocken ed. 1970).

50. J. Mayer, Toward a Non-Malthusian Population Policy, 47 Milbank Mem'l Fund Q. 340-53 (1969).

51. The United States has 22 persons per square kilometer. Austria has 88 and Switzerland 151 and I have found that both these nations provide excellent outdoor recreational activities for its own citizens and numerous tourists. Population density figures from United Nations , supra note 21 at 118, 120, 121.

52. Speech by Barry Commoner delivered to American Academy for the Advancement of Science in Chicago, Ill., December 27, 1970.

53. Speech by Ansley J. Coale delivered to American Academy for the Advancement of Science in Chicago, Ill., December 27, 1970.

54. A. Coale, Population and Economic Development, in THE POPULATION DILEMMA (Hauser ed., 2nd ed., 1969).

55. G. Jones, The Economic Effect of Declining Fertility in Less Developed Countries (occasional paper of the Population Council, 1969).

56. G. Jones, id. at 25-6.

57. Hutchinson, supra note 26.

58. The United States has 22 persons per square kilometer while South Vietnam has 103 and North Vietnam 134. The Soviet Union has 11 people per square kilometer while Czechoslovakia has 113. United Nations, supra note 21, at 115-22.

59. The United Kingdom has 228 persons to the square kilometer and Japan has 277. Id. at pp. 115-22.
The final report of the National Commission on the Causes and Prevention of Violence stated that "...the five cities with the highest metropolitan violent crime rate in 1968 - Baltimore, Newark, Washington, San Francisco, and Detroit - had smaller populations than some very large cities with somewhat lower rates of violent crimes" (a) and yet all these cities, except for Washington whose population remained stable, declined in population during the last decade. (b) During the last ten years New York's population declined by 0.1%(c) while the cities' homicide rate tripled. (d)

    a. National Commission on the Cause and Prevention of Violence, To Establish Justice, To Insure Domestic Tranquility 20 (1969).

    b. Preliminary census reports quoted from U.S. News and World Report, Sept. 17, 1970, p. 24.

    c. Ibid.

    d. N.Y. Times, March 28, 1971, p. 61, col. 3.

60. H. Hoagland, Cybernetics of Population Control, in HUMAN FERTILITY AND POPULATION PROBLEMS (Greep ed. 1963).

61. Life, Feb. 20, 1970, pp. 58-62.

62. Encyclopedia of Social Sciences 26; see N. Himes supra note 49 at 55.

63. F. Hicks, Human Jettison 275-76 (1927). In United States v. Holmes, 26 F. Cas. 360 (CCED Pa., 1842), the Defendant who jettisoned passengers from a lifeboat was convicted only of manslaughter and sentenced to serve six months in prison and paid a fine of $20.00.

64. J. Swift, A Modest Proposal, Swift's Prose Writings 229 (Lane-Poole ed. 1884); M. Mannes, They (1970); Sir William Gilbert wrote in the Mikado, "As some day it might happen that a victim need be found, I've got a little list..." The list was lengthy, indeed. A Treasury of Gilbert and Sullivan 257 (Taylor ed. 1941).

65. Silving, Euthanasia: A Study in Comparative Criminal Law 103 U. Pa. L. Rev. 350 (1954).

66. For example, the United States in 1967 had an infant mortality rate of 22.4 compared to Sweden's 12.9, Denmark's 15.8, or Great Britain's 18.9. United Nations, supra note 21, at 576-79.

67. B. Viel, The Social Consequences of Population Growth, (Population Reference Bureau, 1969)

68. L. Day, The Population Problem in the United States, reprinted in Hearings, supra note 5, at 152-157.

69. D. Harkavy, F. Jaffe, and S. Wishik, Family Planning and Public Policy: Who Is Misleading Whom? 165 SCIENCE 367 (1969), reprinted in Hearings, supra note 5, at 211.

70. W. Peterson, Population 522-23 (2d ed. 1969).

71. See People v. Chavez, 77 Cal. App. 2d. 621, 176 P. 2d 92 (1947).

72. See e.g. Hale v. Manion, 189 Kan. 143, 368 P.2d. 1 (1962); Peterson v. Nationwide Mutual Ins. Co., 175 Ohio St. 551, 197 N.E. 2d 194 (1964).

73. N.Y. Estates, Powers and Trusts Law Sec. 6-5, 7. See 5 American Law of Property Secs. 22.42 - 22.46.

74. Perkins, Criminal Law 101 (1957); Means, The Law of New York Concerning Abortion and the Status of the Fetus, 1664-1968: A Case of Cessation of Constitutionality, 14 N.Y.L.F. 411, 419-22 (1968).

75. See People v. Belous, supra note 17.

76. See H. Cark, Law As An Instrument of Population Control, 40 Colo. L. Rev. 179, 188 (1968).

77. Boston Globe, Dec. 3, 1970, p. 15, col. 3.

78. The population of the United States increased from 201,177,000 in 1968 to 203, 213,000 in 1969. For the year 1968 births exceeded deaths by 1,595,000. U.S. Dept. of Commerce, Statistical Abstract of the United States 1970 5-6 (1970).

79. D. Harkavy, F. Jaffe, and S. Wishik, supra note 69, at 211.

80. See N.Y. Times, May 13, 1970, p. 37, col. 3.

81. L. Cisler, Abortion Reform: The New Tokenism reprinted in RAMPARTS, March 1970, p. 19.

82. D. Callahan, Abortion: Law, Choice and Morality 290 (1970).

83. 12 deaths occurred during the first 69,000 abortions performed under recently enacted New York Abortion law. N.Y. Times, Feb. 7, 1971, p. 70, col. 3. This rate of close to 18 deaths per 100,000 approaches the maternal death rate and greatly exceeds abortion mortality rates of most countries with both permissive abortion laws and adequate medical resources. Most East European countries and Japan have fewer than five deaths per 100,000 abortions. Callahan, id at 287. However, these initially high complication rates have declined drastically in the second half of the year ... as physicians, hospitals and clinics have gained experience and as a greater percentage of women have sought abortion in the first 12 weeks of pregnancy. Pakter and Nelson, Abortion in New York City: The First Nine Months, 3 Family Planning Perspectives No. 3 (July, 1971) pp. 5-6.

84. Baird v. Eisenstadt 429 F. 2d 1398 (1st Cir. 1970).
aff'd 40 L.W. 4303 (Sup. Ct. March 22, 1972).

85. See Pub. L. No. 91-572 (1970).

86. The following statistics were compiled by the Rockefeller Foundation and published in the Boston Globe, Dec. 3,
1970, p. 1, col. 3.

COMPARISON OF CONTRACEPTIVE METHODS

One Year with 1 million women age 24-35 using each method

METHOD	NUMBER OF PREGNANCIES	DEATHS DUE TO PREGNANCIES	DEATHS DUE TO CONTRACEPTIVES	TOTAL DEATHS
NOTHING	880,000	200	0	200
I.U.D.	30,000	7	2	9
PILL	5,000	1	13	14
DIAPHRAGM	120,000	27	0	27
RHYTHM	240,000	55	0	55

87. A warning that the pill may be hazardous to one's
health may be terribly misleading to a woman during her fertile
years since the failure to use the pill may be more hazardous.
See Chart reproduced above. Recent polls indicate that many
women have abandoned or are contemplating abandoning the
pill as a result of certain disclosures concerning its potential
hazards. Given present statistics, this recent exercise in
"consumer protection" may prove counterproductive.

88. 204 Journal of the American Medical Ass'n. 821
(1968).

89. N.Y. Times, April 8, 1970, p. 1., col. 2.

90. Dr. N. Fiumara, Director of the Division of Communicable and Venereal Diseases of the Massachusetts Department of Public Health states "that gonorrhea and syphilis in the U.S. has increased by 1000 percent among teenagers over the past five years." N.Y. Times, Jan., 3, 1971, p. 25., col. 1.

91. Lee, Law and Family Planning, Background Paper Prepared for the Expert Committee on Family Planning in Health Services World Health Organization 17-30 (1970).

92. D. Heer, Society and Population 9 (1968); W. Langer, Europe Initial Population Explosion, in Readings on Population, 9-10 (Heer ed. 1968).
For example, many factors contributed to dramatic fall in the marriage rate and the rise in the median age of marriage that occurred in Ireland from the mid-nineteenth century until the present. Economic deprivation, inability of young males to establish an independent economic base, and strict sanctions against contraception lead many Irishmen to delay marriage or embrace celibacy. See Peterson, supra note 70, at 514-17.

93. U.S. Dept. of Commerce, supra note 78, at 60.

94. Improved contraception and more readily-available abortion enable couples to conduct sexual relations without having to risk bearing an unwanted child. A growing acceptance of pre-marital sex should relieve some of the pressures for early marriage.

95. Congress recently lowered the minimum voting age from 21 to 18 in both Federal and State elections. P. L. 91-285, 84 Stat. 314. This law was held constitutional as it applies to elections for Federal officials. Oregon v. Mitchell, 91 S. Ct. 260 (1970).

96. See J. Blake, Social Structure and Fertility, Economic Development and Cultural Change 226 (1966).

97. N.Y. Times, Dec. 7, 1970, p. 1., col. 1.

98. L. Day and A. Day, Too Many Americans (1964), reprinted Hearings, supra note 5, at 186; J. Blake, Popula-

tion Policy for Americans: Is the Government Being Misled? 164 Science 522 (1969), reprinted in Hearings, supra note 5, at 217.

99. J. Sweet, Family Composition and the Labor Force Activity of American Wives, 7 DEMOGRAPHY 208 (1970).

100. Int. Rev. Code of 1954, Sec. 151, amended by Pub. L. No. 91-172 (1969), increasing the amount of the deduction.

101. Int. Rev. Code of 1954, Sec. 2.

102. Under Sec. 214 of the Int. Rev. Code of 1954, no child care expenses would be allowed as a deduction if the combined income of both husband and wife exceed $6000.00. For taxable years after 1971, child care provisions have been liberalized. Pub. L. 92-178, Sec. 210(a).

103. A married man with taxable income of $20,000 who files a joint return pays $4380 in taxes. This is an effective tax rate of approximately 21%. If his wife enters the labor force, the first dollar of her income will be taxed at an effective rate of 32%.

104. About 23 million of 65.4 million individual income tax returns for the year 1965 had adjusted gross income of $5000 - 10,000. Of these only 3.3 million were filed by single persons. U.S. Treasury Dept. Statistics of Income 1965, Individual Income Tax Returns 2 (1967).

105. Authorities cited note 70, supra.

106. In Dandridge v. Williams, 397 U.S. 471 (1970) the Court upheld the Maryland welfare law which limited the maximum amount of welfare benefits available to any family irrespective of the number of children in the family.

107. D. Harkavy, F. Jaffe, S. Wishik, supra note 69, at 208.

108. Declaration on Population: The World Leaders Statement, 26 Studies in Family Planning 1-3 (January, 1968).

PART TWO

The Forum Proceedings

Donald T. Fox

The Special Committee on the Lawyer's Role in the Search for Peace was established in 1961 with the authority and the duty to develop and carry out a program to promote the education of the Bar and to stimulate discussion among lawyers with respect to problems of peace and the lawyer's role in the search for peace.

This is a big role which, practically speaking, has been especially difficult to carry out since losing our outside source of funding. Nevertheless, with the cooperation of public spirited scholars, the committee has been able to arrange a distinguished series of programs under the title of "The Hammarskjöld Forums". The proceedings of these forums, published by Oceana Publications, Inc., have become useful reference works.

If you attended past Hammarskjöld Forums or read these publications, our topic for tonight may appear to be unusual. Traditionally, we have dealt with legal aspects of critical problems in the foreign relations of the United States. Tonight, instead of a specific foreign crisis, we decided to deal with the broad topic of population policy.

Our reasons for doing so are twofold: In the first place, it seemed to us that what Professor Ehrlich calls "the population bomb" has come to rank with atomic weapons as a widely feared engine of potential world disaster. The most recent edition of the United Nations Demographic Yearbook predicts that if current trends continue, world population will double to 7 billion people in the next 36 years. Dr. Norman Borlaug referred to this growth rate on the occasion of receiving a Nobel Prize for his contributions to expanding food production in developing countries. He said that continuation of population growth will lead to destruction of the human species.

Likewise, the President of the World Bank has taken every occasion to stress the need for immediate action to reduce the present birth rate. His most recent annual report emphasized the following conclusion of the Pearson Committee: "No other phenomenon casts a darker shadow over prospects for interna-

tional development than the staggering growth of population....
It is clear that there can be no serious social and economic
planning unless the ominous implications of uncontrolled population growth are understood and acted upon."

Our Special Committee, we believe, represents a segment
of the Bar that is relatively enlightened and well-informed on
problems of international significance. However, we found ourselves totally unprepared to evaluate these increasingly alarming predictions about uncontrolled population growth. We know
that President Nixon recently signed legislation on family planning which he hailed as a "landmark" population bill. We know
that Senator Packwood has introduced legislation to stabilize
the United States population through means including tax incentives for smaller families. But, although scientists in many
fields were reporting on possible effects of increasing population
on the prospects for a stable world order, we were not well
enough informed to react intelligently to these alarms.

In view of the seriousness with which other disciplines
viewed population growth as an international problem, we thought
that the members of this Association and a wider segment of the
Bar generally should be better informed about the dimensions of
this phenomenon so that the tools of our profession could be
brought to bear more effectively on the development of population policy.

In beginning a movement in this direction, we have been ex-
traordinarily fortunate in that four of the world's most widely
respected experts on population policy agreed to appear on tonight's forum.

Furthermore, one of the few members of our profession who
has given sustained thought to the legal aspects of population
policy agreed to prepare a working paper for tonight's forum.
This document, which I hope most of you have read, will serve
as the basis for our program. Professor Donald Berman of
the Northeastern University School of Law will begin our forum
by summarizing the conclusions of his paper. Thereupon, I will
ask each of the panel members to address himself briefly to an
aspect of Professor Berman's paper. Following this, a colloquy
will ensue among Professor Berman, the members of the panel
and you in the audience.

At this time it gives me great pleasure to introduce the author of the working paper, Professor Donald Berman of Northeastern University.

Professor Berman

First of all, I do not view population as a polemical issue. I take strong exception to people like Paul Ehrlich--the great prophets of doom. I am somewhat optimistic because I view the problem with a lawyer's skepticism. The fear mongers just haven't proven to me that I should be pessimistic yet.

The first basic conclusion that I draw after having studied this field at some length is that demographers have a difficult time telling us precisely how many people we now have in the world. It's true they can make some fairly accurate estimates, but they could be off by several percentage points, expecially since we have no clearly reliable figures from Communist China, the world's largest nation, containing approximately one quarter of the world's population. But where the trick comes into this whole business is trying to predict how many people we will have tomorrow or ten years from now or fifty years from now.

This requires that the demographer predict future fertility patterns - not how many children we are having today, but the number of children people will have ten years from now, fifteen years from now, fifty years hence. In this endeavor demographers have been notoriously inaccurate. Indeed, two decades ago, people were still talking in terms of the extinction of the race from depopulation. Two decades before that they were talking about overpopulation. And now it seems to be fashionable today to talk about the population bomb. Now, I am not saying that the bomb won't explode. I'm only saying that there is strong evidence that the bomb will be defused.

I think you have to distinguish fairly clearly the developed nations, such as the United States, that have passed through the different phases of demographic transition. I can say with some confidence that the United States has its population problem pretty much under control. We have, I think, fairly widespread family planning services that will be made available to all our citizens. There is a major assault on barriers to voluntary abortion, which I believe will be successful and will result in the elimination of virtually all of the unwanted pregnancies in the United States. I also believe that inflation and the general problems of living in a highly complex urban society, are, in fact, leading Americans to desire fewer children. So that when we talk about the United States, I think that we are talking about a problem that is materially different than the problem of, let's say, India or Pakistan or Latin America.

Now, even when you get to the underdeveloped nations of the world, there exists evidence that given a certain chemistry -- and God knows what that is -- even these nations are capable of experiencing sharp, dramatic reductions in fertility patterns. In countries like Taiwan, South Korea, Singapore, there have been dramatic reductions in the fertility rate. And if these patterns were to continue, there would be the unity of reproduction rate, that is, you'd have enough births only to cover the deaths by the turn of the century. There is no reason for me to believe that this kind of change will not come about in a number of the other underdeveloped countries. I am not saying that that change has yet come about, and I am not trying to tell this audience that there is not a real problem in India and Pakistan.

The only point that I want to make is that when we talk about seriously encroaching upon what a great many people believe to be a fundamental right, that is, to choose the number of children one wants to bear, that when you start encroaching on that right, even by economic incentives, you should be fairly sure that a disaster is going to occur, because you are asking the poor to bear a disproportionate burden in the war on population.

A very simple example and then I will close. A denial of an income tax exemption for a third child in the United States, which is Senator Packwood's proposal, would, by 1973, when the dependency exemption will be $750, cost the 50 percent bracket taxpayer $350, which is 7/10 of 1 percent of his $50,000 a year annual income, an insignificant amount. A poor man with taxable income of $2,000 a year who is in the 15 percent bracket, loses only $112.50 when he foregoes a $750 exemption, but this amounts to over 5 percent of his annual income.

When you begin to examine how these various economic incentive programs will work, (for example, payment in exchange for sterilization) you will confront the poor man with an onerous choice not faced by the more affluent. I rebel against this.

I would like to make one other point. Neither in the underdeveloped nations of the world, nor in the United States, have we presented to the population an educational program in conjunction with the delivery of family planning services. It is still not possible in the United States for everyone to obtain the most sophisticated contraceptive methods and abortion.

We have not even begun to exhaust the policies of education. Before we move to anything more coercive that the mere choice being given and an educational program designed to bring to the public the full range of choices available to them, I would oppose any other type of measure, including such things as cutting off welfare payments or the limitation of tax deductions.

The only thing I would stress is the educational program and giving the people the ability to make up their own minds by the availability of family planning services and abortion.

Chairman Fox

With that succinct resume of conclusions, we will now turn to a discussion of the issues raised in the working paper by four distinguished scientists. To begin, I would like to introduce Dr. Christopher Tietze, who graduated from the University of Vienna Medical School and practiced in that city until 1938. Emigrating to the United States, he was associated with the mental hygiene study at John Hopkins and later became chief of the population and labor staff in the Department of State. From 1958 to 1966 he was Director of Research of the National Committee of Maternal Health, and is now with the Bio-Medical Division of The Population Council. Dr. Tietze serves on the boards of directors of the Association of the Study of Abortion, and on Governor Rockefeller's Advisory Committee on Abortion. He has served on several scientific groups of the World Health Organization concerned with human reproduction. He is the author of more than 155 articles in the field of demography and the control of human fertility.

Dr. Tietze

First of all, I would like to say that I agree with what I take to be Professor Berman's main thesis, to wit, that in the United States the role of population growth as an aggravating factor in the various ills that beset the republic is sufficiently small and sometimes obscure as to make any resort to coercive measures inappropriate at this time.

On this basic issue there is no disagreement between our speaker and myself. I feel very strongly that such coercive measures should not be undertaken until--unless and until--all voluntary methods have been tried. And it is simply not true that in the United States we have had both the legal facilities and the delivery system which would make it possible for all couples to have only those children which they actually want.

I am not entirely sure that I would agree with Professor Berman in his definition of what he calls coercive. If I understand him correctly, he would extend this term to cover a broad variety of measures which other people perhaps would call persuasive. But he would not include education, which can amount to a very powerful sort of coercion by brainwashing.

It would seem to me that our customs contain a great many elements which are in favor of a higher rate of reproduction, and I would like him to expound on the question of the extent to which our laws contain pro-natalist elements. If he is opposed to the introduction of anti-natalist elements short of physical coercion, I would suspect that he would take a very dim view of the pro-natalist elements in our legal system.

I also believe that -- and perhaps I am speaking with a certain amount of hurt professional pride -- that Professor Berman has been a little bit too harsh on demographers. Surely our estimates of the world population may be off by a 100 million or by 200 million, but even 200 million would be only 6 per cent and that I submit, is a pretty good estimate.

While it is true that we cannot predict with any real accuracy what the fertility pattern will be in this country or any other country to the end of the century, there are some things which we can say. We can say that given existing levels of mortality and assuming that the generation of women now entering reproductive life will, as of now, limit themselves to an average family of two children, even then under this hypothetical assumption, our total population would have to grow by about 25 to 30 percent to the end of the century. There is no way, short of catastrophe, this could be avoided. Moreover, I do not see the slightest indication that women now entering the childbearing period will, in fact, produce only two children on the average. Now this type of growth may not be a catastrophe for the United States, but it will happen.

There are some indications that the expected number of children is going down, that young wives now in their early twenties expect maybe 2.8 children rather than 3.3 children, as women who are in their thirties, but nowhere do I see a drop down to a level of 2.1 which, of course, would represent a zero population growth.

I have great sympathy and great respect for women's liberation. To paraphrase, some of my best friends are women's lib types, but I do not consider them now as a major demographic force. I wish they were, but they aren't.

And I would put it to Professor Berman whether what he proposes, the attitude he takes and the attitude he wants us to take, is what a prudent man would do. I have the impression that Professor Berman is satisfied that we cannot prove that the most favorable course of events will take place. Therefore, there is no need to take any drastic steps. It would seem to me that what the prudent man should do is to weigh the whole situation, to apply the best judgment of which he is capable, and then do one of two things: Either to fashion his action on what he considers the most probable course of events in the foreseeable future, or that course of events which is unfavorable, but still not entirely unreasonable.

It seems to me in our actual lives we are aware of Murphy's law - when anything can go wrong it will go wrong - and we should make assumptions, like public utilities should, that several things will go wrong so that they will still be able to supply the current. I think it is unwise to neglect the balance of evidence and not to consider the probability that certain undesirable effects may occur.

And finally, before closing, I would like to put one other question on the table. It seems to me that while in his paper Professor Berman has referred from time to time to other regions, other parts of the world, essentially he has discussed the question in United States terms. Now there is nothing wrong with it. After all, this is our country and we are first of all concerned with the question here. But it seems that implicit in all he has said is our concept, our American or our Atlantic concept of the proper relationship between the individual and the state and the community. I could imagine that in another social setting -- in mainland China, in the Soviet Union, perhaps even in India, a lawyer would come to an entirely different conclusion in balancing the requirements of individual freedom versus the threat to the community. I repeat that I believe we are not as of now in the United States in a situation where we have to jeopardize individual freedom, but I think we should be explicitly aware that this is not necessarily the case everywhere.

I do not share Professor Berman's optimism as to the success of vigorous family planning programs in a number of countries. I have yet to see a country which would devote to family planning more than a miniscule fraction of governmental expenditure in comparison to what it spends on more conventional expenditures, such as armaments. I certainly am not impressed with the successes in most of the larger countries such as India, Pakistan, Indonesia and many others. True, there have been declines in some countries on the rim of Asia, most of them of a highly urbanized nature, such as Singapore or Hongkong, also in Taiwan and Korea. There is argument among demographers just how much the program has done and how much would have happened anyway. But certainly things are changing very, very slowly in the large countries that really matter.

Chairman Fox

Dr. Tietze has raised some very interesting questions and we are not going to lose sight of them. I think, though, out of concern for my brother lawyer, he would like to ponder them a little bit and get all four barrels of this expert battery before we call on him to give a general reply.

Professor Ansley J. Coale has been a professor of economics and Director of the Office of Population Research at Princeton University since 1959. Professor Coale also has served as United States Representative to the United Nations Population Commission. He has been President of the American Population Association and is author or co-author of a number of distinguished works on a range of problems from reducing vulnerability to atomic bombs to population growth and economic development in low income countries. Among his numerous articles is one on "Man and His Environment" in the October issue of Science Magazine. This article caused him to be deluged with even more than the number of requests to speak which he ordinarily receives and therefore we are particularly grateful that he consented to come from Princeton tonight for this forum.

Dr. Coale

I am really sorry that Professor Berman rather than going into law school didn't at some time decide to come to Princeton or another university and study demography, because, having devoted only one year to studying the subject, in the midst of an otherwise busy career, he is largely a self-taught demographer and has, I think, mastered a great deal and has done an impressive job. Perhaps I feel that way because on many of the principal points he makes I find myself in substantial agreement, and had he differed more I might be less impressed with his demography. Nevertheless, it does seem to me that there are some points with which I can take exception and some other points where I think he could have carried the argument further, and some things that I think he omitted.

-40-

Some of the points with which I differ, points more or less of fact, have already been discussed by Chris Tietze, the most important one being that I think Professor Berman has underestimated the gravity of the prospective population growth in the developing countries. It seems to me uncertain whether there will be a massive decline in fertility in major countries.

There has essentially been no change in fertility that we can be sure of in some of the countries with the highest birth rates and the largest populations in Asia and throughout much of Latin America. It would take a very sanguine estimate indeed to assume that the fertility decline which has, in many instances, not been initiated and in others barely so, that it would get us to a level of about replacement within the next three decades. So it seems to me that there is a more ominous prospect of continuing population growth.

Now I say that without implying that I, myself, advocate coercive measures such as obligatory sterilization or other extreme measures, because I think that in fact even if these populations do grow that does not mean inevitable starvation. I think there have been over-alarmist statements along that line. But even though those prophets of gloom are perhaps overemphatic in their statements, nevertheless, I think we have to acknowledge that continuing population growth in these countries is a barrier to a more rapid progress they so desperately need, and that it is a matter of concern both for those countries and for the community of nations to find ways to hasten the decline of fertility rather than letting nature take its course, so to speak.

Let me turn to what seems to me the issues that were either underemphasized or neglected in the general area of population policy, whether it be with regard to the United States or in the developing countries.

In looking at population policy personally, I tend to put it in steps and I think of policies that I can at the moment subscribe to without question because I can see their implications and see them as overwhelmingly favorable and see them as not being counter to the values that at least I hold, although they are counter to some other people's values. These are the sort of classic planned parenthood objectives of bringing to every couple the possibility that the births or indeed the pregnancies they have are the result of conscious and informed decision; that is, that people do not have children they do not consciously desire to have. And, ideally, that they do not have pregnancies they do not consciously decide to have and that, in making that conscious decision, they have an adequate amount of information about the implications for themselves, their families, the children and perhaps even for their societies.

Now that seems to me to be an objective of population policy that most people can subscribe to, although there are people who have religious objections. And I would want, myself, to go one step further and advocate a society in which when accidental pregnancies occur, the couple can terminate them through an abortion which is available on request under medically safe auspices and at a price that they can afford. That's much more controversial. There are lots of people who would disagree and doubtless there are legal issues involved on which there would be disagreement. One of the reasons I feel that way is that I think the implications for the child who is born when he is an unwanted child are unfavorable from the outset and often not apt to get much better.

So that although not all can agree with this direction of policy toward freeing people from unwanted births, and certainly if abortion is included there will be a lot of disagreement, nevertheless it is a direction that is increasingly acceptable to many segments of our society and many others. But the difficulty is that I think it is an article of faith to assume that if we had such a utopia in terms of planned parenthood policies, that is, if we had a utopia in which every pregnancy was an intended one, the result would be a socially optimal or even necessarily a socially acceptable level of births.

How do we know, other than having some notion about Adam Smith's invisible hand, that the result would be that everyone would, let's say, have the number of children needed for replacement, and in the long run that's what any society must have. That is, we can't have a continued geometric increase of population in any society, because as I have often calculated, it only takes a calculable number of years for population to have one person per square foot or to outweigh the earth and reach other ridiculous outcomes, if it continues to grow even at a rather slow rate indefinitely.

So that in the long run the only rate of increase which is socially advantageous or socially possible is a zero rate, and if we want to achieve that in conjunction with the kinds of low mortality that are achievable today, that means that we must have small families.

Now what I am saying is that there is no social law and no logical reason to suppose that every individual couple deciding on the number of children they want and having made an informed decision about it will produce an average of 2.1, which is what would be needed for replacement.

I think that it is not a good form of public policy that people should be asked to shape their individual decisions to fit the public welfare. Rather, I think society should set rules and conditions so that in pursuing their self-interest, people will be led to that position.

I remember an economist colleague of mine saying that Adam Smith showed that, in the field of economic production, competition led people to produce what was socially desirable. We have great doubts about that since Adam Smith invented the phrase of the invisible hand as leading to this result, and my economist friend said that political science should be the artificial creation of invisible hands.

What we need is a policy that will lead people to have a number of children that in the aggregate will be the socially desirable number or the socially essential number in the long run. And that seems not necessarily to involve coercion. In fact, I would hope it wouldn't, and I think it should not, but it seems to me that Professor Berman dismissed too readily all forms of incentives as being coercive.

An example is this: In another area which is less fraught with emotion, the question of monetary control in an effort to influence the course of price, inflation and employment, even the President has come to accept the notion that our monetary and fiscal policy should be directed to those ends. And we don't say that an individual should not spend his salary, that it is unpatriotic and wrong for him to spend his salary because it leads to inflation. We don't ask individuals voluntarily to send in contributions to the government to offset inflation. We set a tax rate, and then we allow people to spend their income, save and invest as they choose, within a tax rate which is set to prevent runaway inflation or severe unemployment.

I would submit that if we ever achieve a time when every individual couple had only the pregnancies that they had voluntarily chosen, then we could try to affect a marginal decision whether to have another pregnancy or not in a way that would conform to what was socially desirable.

I share with Professor Berman the opposition to Senator Packwood's bill, although I think he miscalculated in saying how bad it was for the poor by not allowing for effective exemptions.

A man of $2,000 doesn't pay any taxes, if he has a family of four. Anyway, that was a detail. I, nevertheless, share the opposition to that bill and to other laws that are punitive now, because the punitive law that withheld welfare benefits and so on, would fall exactly on the unwanted children and on the children in the families that are already excessively large. They already suffer deprivation and disadvantages and that would merely increase it.

It seems to me that would be unacceptably inequitable. We have a child who is born and is sixth now and is unwanted and we tell his parents that they have to pay some kind of financial penalty. The child, as I say, already gets an inadequate education and probably is abused by his parents psychologically and otherwise because he was unwanted. Now they have to pay a penalty on top and that certainly wouldn't make him any more welcome.

I don't think when a large proportion of pregnancies are unwanted that we can easily have coercive and punitive measures. But if we achieve the primary goal that I think is one that all societies can already work for, then I think it would not be inequitable to have fringe payments and penalties to bring the social cost of having children in line with the individual cost, impose more of the social cost upon the individual couple.

Chairman Fox

Following that illuminating comment by Professor Coale on the possibility of a population policy which conduces toward a socially acceptable level of births without coercion, I would like to introduce another of our experts, whose position requires him to take a world view of population problems.

Halvor Gille studied economics at the University of Copenhagen before working in the fields of population and social development with the Swedish and Danish Governments. He entered the United Nations Population Division in 1950 and served as Chief of the Division of Social Affairs in the Economic Commission for Asia and the Far East. From 1963 to 1969 he was the director of the Division of Social Affairs of the United Nations Office for Europe and is now Associate Director of the United Nations Fund for Population Activities. He has written a number of articles, the most recent of which is "Population" in a publication entitled International Targets for Development.

Mr. Gille

It has been a great pleasure for me to read Professor Berman's stimulating paper. I think he has very clearly stated his points of view and maybe sometimes overstated them in order to stimulate a discussion, but I think that is welcome.

I find myself to be in a very large extent in agreement with the two previous speakers on the panel in believing that Professor Berman has maybe been too pessimistic about population predictions and the role they can play, but on the other hand has been too optimistic about the impact of family planning programs.

I would like, Mr. Chairman, to limit myself to the problems in developing countries and not speak on the situation in the United States. I had a feeling that Professor Berman had to a very large extent the problems in this country in mind and that he may not have given enough allowance for the tremendous differences between the situation in this country and that in developing countries, and the differences in conditions between developing countries and very often even within each developing country.

Now on the population projections, I am not defending them because they are United Nations projections, but I do feel that they have served a useful purpose and we could not have done without them. I think the criticisms often made against the population projections are based upon the bad experience of such projections in highly developed countries. Of course, in a way, it's even more difficult to make population projections for developing countries because the information you have -- your starting point, the current rate of fertility and mortality, the interrelationships between social-economic factors and demographic factors -- such information is certainly far more limited in developing countries.

But on the other hand, we should remember that for most of the developing countries the difficulty in estimating the future levels of fertility may not be so great if you take a liberal attitude. At present, in most of these countries, the level of fertility is high and is constant and the problem is, of course, to determine the timing and at what rate the level of fertility will decline. On the mortality side, we are a little better off. It's not so difficult, I think, to estimate the expected future mortality decline and furthermore this doesn't have the same great impact upon the age factor in population.

The fact is certainly that we know quite well the expected or projected population figures for the adult population and for the labor force, which in itself is, of course, an important thing. It should not be overlooked. We know that the working population in the developing world will double before the end of the century irrespective of what happens to fertility. We know that the annual increase in the working population will double in the course of the decade of the 1970's and will be three times higher than it is today by the end of the century. We also know that new jobs have to be created for almost half of the newcomers in the developing countries today and new jobs have to be created for around two-thirds of all the newcomers in less than ten years in these countries.

There is a tremendous force in the rate of population growth which Professor Coale has already referred to, which should not be ignored. In India today, for every woman leaving the reproductive age group, two to two and a half women will take her place entering the reproductive age group.

Now on family planning programs and the impact of family planning programs, I said that I believe that Professor Berman is too optimistic, unfortunately. Professor Coale has already mentioned that there are very few instances of success. They are all rather specialized cases -- urban areas, small populations -- or the trend of fertility was already going down at the time when national family planning programs were introduced. That is not to say that these programs had no impact, but it has been rather difficult to determine to what extent these programs have had an impact and to what extent the decline would have occurred in any case to some extent, due to economic and social forces.

Now Professor Berman believes that, as he said, given availability of certain chemistry it should not be difficult to accomplish rapid decline in fertility. He indicated in his paper that he believes improved contraception, cheaper abortion methods and ways of determining fetal sex will greatly reduce fertility in developing countries. I don't think it's so easy. First of all, we do not have today suitable, effective, acceptable methods appropriate for large groups of the population in developing countries.

Cheap abortion methods, yes, we may have that now, but abortion is generally not acceptable, at least not in most of the Asian countries and African countries. So it would take some time before this method could be applied, and even then it would be rather difficult keeping in mind the fact that the rural population, which constitutes often 70 to 80 percent of the total population in these countries, is scarcely covered by health services, medical personnel, and so on.

About methods of determining fetal sex, I don't think we have that method yet and I think it's a long way until we do. I don't think that we need to speculate about that.

Now on national programs, there is a large number of programs, more than 30 developing countries have fully committed to family programing as a part of their development policies and as part of their planning for economic or social development. But the impact is very limited, except for the few cases we have referred to earlier.

Let's take the most serious case, India. The living conditions are almost the lowest anywhere in the world. India was the first country to start a national family planning program and has given it serious attention, with very large inputs from internal and external sources. And still today certainly not more than 10 percent of the population is covered by these services. Most of that population you will find in urban areas and a few limited rural areas where there have been special circumstances or where there have been very extensive inputs. So according to the best governmental estimates, the birth rate has declined from 41 per thousand to 39 per thousand. And that is the change which has taken place in approximately the last ten years.

Now about incentives and the human right to determine family size, I also feel like Professor Coale that the author of the working paper has been too critical about incentives. The famous transistor radios you so often hear about, they never existed. It was a proposal made by the Indian Minister of State for Family Planning, but he didn't get very far with his proposal, and it was never introduced.

When we talk about incentives in the field of family planning, we talk usually about monetary incentives in order to persuade couples to come forward to obtain advice. To overcome some economic handicaps they may have, they may need to take a couple of days off and they need to have payment of transport, lodging and so on. Many programs do have this kind of incentive. And I think there are other forms of incentives. You could provide food to families interested in family planning. I really see no harm in such an approach.

I don't agree with Professor Berman that this means encroachment upon human rights. Is it a human right to remain poor, to be unable to limit family size, to be unable to care for children already born? I am not so sure it is. If this human right you talk about for developing countries should mean anything, it should be an obligation of governments to make facilities available to assist families to at least attain their wishes, to protect the health of minors and children, and to improve the well being of families. Only in those terms, I think , may the human right become meaningful.

We have to remember that even if we take the situation and the attitudes as they are at present in most rural populations in developing countries, where they want a family size of around three to four surviving children, this will mean that even if we are able to help them to attain this goal, the rate of population growth will be around 2 to 2.5 percent per annum in these countries. And it really means a fairly modest relief in the pressure upon educational facilities, upon housing, upon employment, upon total services and so on in these countries.

Now, Mr. Chairman, in concluding I just want to raise one point. I don't want to miss this opportunity in addressing a group of lawyers to urge you to focus upon the problems in many countries, not only in this country. I would like to encourage you to help developing countries in particular to review and examine various laws, social and economic, and to help them bring them more into line with population objectives which the governments may have established. There are a very large number of examples of laws in countries committed to a family planning program which run counter to the objectives of a national family planning program. Very often they are accustomed to import contraceptives, but laws at least make it difficult to distribute, sell and advertise contraceptives. There are laws which could be improved in order to raise the age of marriage and so on. I think lawyers have a responsibility in trying from their point of view to assist toward the goals which the governments may have established.

Chairman Fox

We accept that responsibility Mr. Gille and, with the assistance of programs like this to heighten the concern and increase the knowledge of the legal profession about population policy, maybe we can arrive at a point at which we can discharge it.

At this time, I would like to introduce another distinguished foreign member of our panel. Dr. Benjamin Viel took his initial medical training in Chile and then obtained masters and doctoral degrees in public health from Harvard and Johns Hopkins, respectively. From 1952 to 1962, he was the director of the Medical School at the University of Chile and has been a visiting professor at many universities in North and South America, as well as in Great Britain, Russia and Israel. He has received a number of awards for his publications, which include three books and over 35 articles. One of his great distinctions is that of having planned and supervised one of the most successful programs in making family planning available to the poor. This program in Santiago, Chile, has been widely studied as a model of what is achievable in this field. At present Dr. Viel is Director General of the Western Hemisphere Region, International Planned Parenthood Federation.

Dr. Viel

Basically, I agree with Dr. Tietze that there is a completely different problem in developed countries than there is in underdeveloped countries. And if there is a reason to be optimistic about the future of the population problem in the developed countries, there is not any reason at all to be optimistic about what's going to happen in the underdeveloped world.

Speaking of Latin America, I must say that without exception the law in Latin America is pro-natalistic. From severe penalties for infanticide or induced abortion to increased salaries for each living child, as well as tax deductions for family dependents, all our present legislation encourages population increase.

All legislation in Latin America was approved in relation to this problem in the middle of the last century. The social conditions in that period of our life justified the attitude of the legislators. A vast land had to be occupied and conquered. The human muscle was the only source of energy. All these factors were demanding an increase in population, especially considering that the newborn were born in a vast environment and in a time in which we lacked knowledge of how to control communicable disease. But that old legislation is still in force and is applied now to a completely different society.

Today, most of the available land is already under production and if there is any virgin land still left in Latin America it would require a considerable amount of capital to put it into work. The human muscle has been successfully replaced by machine. Besides, there is much better medical care and the major infectious diseases have been controlled. Due to these new conditions, the death rate has declined since 1930.

Latin America has now an average population growth rate of nearly three percent per year. Such a speed has never been observed in the history of humanity.

It is logical that women have reacted against the law and are now practicing all over Latin America illegally induced abortion. Such a condition is reaching epidemic proportions; in Chile alone the cost of complications ensuing from illegally induced abortion is $1 million per year. In a country of 9 million people the national health service is spending that amount of money only in the treatment of complicated cases of induced illegal abortion.

We know that there is a certain amount of infanticide, but we do not know and we cannot put into numbers what I like to call the unconscious infanticide. There are certain facts that prove to me that such a condition exists. For instance, in the poorer district of the City of Santiago, we have found that in families with two children the infant mortality was 60 per thousand. In families of similar social and economic conditions that have ten children, infant mortality was 300 per thousand, or five times greater.

In a careful analysis that we finished at the end of last year in a well baby clinic that we have, thanks to the generosity of Macy Foundation, we found that the punctuality of mothers in taking children to the clinic, breast feeding and general care for the children, declined steadily with the number of children. Good mothers for the first two children become very poor mothers to the fourth or fifth child in the same family under the same roof. With those facts I am inclined to believe that the so-called maternal instinct is not in existence, and if it exists, that it declines according to the number of children.

With such a picture it seems to me that the only hope for a continent like Latin America is, as Professor Berman says, education, with laws that help the educators and doctors to provide families with the means to have the children that they really want. That could be the ideal. But even if some day we reach that ideal we must consider that these conditions have existed for at least 30 years, and that strong measures must be taken now to help existing mothers who were not educated or who did not receive courses in sex education or family planning when they were in school. Now they are at the reproductive age. We must reach them. And that demands a special program. If we do not meet this demand, we are not going to reach any substantial decline in our birth rate.

The point that I would like to emphasize is that those who are working now in Latin America in any kind of program related to family planning are working against the law and all our legislation forbids us to distribute contraceptives, to use them or even to educate about them. The medical profession and the educators are being completely abandoned by the lawyers in this respect. To me it is especially gratifying to see that a group of lawyers here in New York could cooperate to open the eyes of the legal profession in Latin America in that respect.

Chairman Fox

Thank you, Dr. Viel, for that eloquent statement of the population problem in Latin America.

Professor Berman, there are a number of qualified and concerned people in the audience who have questions to ask. Before we get to that stage, a number of specific questions have been raised by members of the panel to which you may wish to respond, entering into such dialogue with them as you thought would be helpful before we went on to the question period.

Professor Berman

Actually, Mr. Gille is right in one respect. When I wrote this paper I did try to overstate my case in order to stimulate discussion. After hearing the panelists I am becoming more convinced that I stated the truth. At least I stated the truth in terms of where I think we should be going as far as world population policy is concerned.

I do agree with Dr. Tietze that education can be coercive if it approaches brainwashing. I am not suggesting a program of brainwashing. I am only suggesting that freeing people to make a decision requires education. It's hard to make intelligent decisions if you are not educated as to the various possibilities. To my knowledge, vast numbers of people in the United States and greater numbers throughout the world have not been subjected to the two basic elements of voluntary family planning. That is, education and the availability of the service, including contraception and abortion. It seems to me absolutely clear that before we start talking about any other form of attack on the population problem, we owe it to the people whose tax deductions are going to be taken away, we owe it to them to first

-51-

give them the opportunity to be educated and to have available family planning services, including abortion.

I am in total agreement with everything that Dr. Viel has said, that it is an obligation on the part of lawyers to struggle even in the United States with our restrictive practices on the availability of abortion, for example. It seems to me absolutely clear that in this country and in other areas of the world we must remove all those pro-natalist laws which are directly related to the birth control problem; for example, import duties on contraceptive devices. It seems clear to me that the clinics operating in Chile and other nations in the world should not be operating illegally.

The thing I am concerned about is bringing the hand of the state to bear in a detrimental way on the part of those people who already have the law operating on them in so many onerous ways. In other words, any type of economic incentive program inevitably will work against the large family which already is at a subsistence level.

Dr. Tietze was interested in the degree to which our present laws are pro-natalist, that is, by encouraging high fertility rates. I am in favor of changing those laws, even though I may not be in favor of introducing anti-natalist laws. I think this is a semantic discussion because if you favor one you probably will oppose the other.

Let us consider a few of the laws that seem to affect fertility, such as the age of marriage. I would not be in favor of raising the age of marriage in the United States, even though most demographers agree that increasing the age of marriage tends to decrease fertility. I am against it because it is inconsistent with everything else we are trying to do as far as bringing young people into the governing of the society. For years we have said if you are old enough to fight you are old enough to vote. Now some people are saying that if they are old enough to vote and old enough to fight, they should be able to marry.

In addition, about one-fifth to one-third of all brides are going to the altar pregnant, suggesting another way in which increasing the age of marriage would increase the hardship on people in society.

Let us also note our tax policy, which is also pro-natalist. The joint return, for example, has the effect of encouraging early marriage. It also has the effect of taxing each dollar of the working wife's income at the marginal rate of the husband. So that the effective tax rate on the husband's income is somewhat lower than the effective rate of the working wife's income. It would take me a little while to spell this out with the figures, but it is apparent that the joint return may be pro-natalist also because it encourages people to marry early in order to get a more favorable overall tax rate.

However, we have had a disastrous experience in this country with the separate return from the standpoint of tax policy. For example, the community property laws in the State of California co-exist with separate property in New York. So New Yorkers were taxed at a rate less favorable than Californians. Before the joint return you had ingenious income splitting devices, such as wives employed as phony directors of corporations. To deal with the community property-separate property problem, states like Pennsylvania and Michigan, I believe, abandoned separate property for community property systems. This raised havoc, so, finally, Congress responded and adopted the joint federal return. I would be opposed to repealing the joint return because I think the cost in tax policy greatly outweighs whatever might be the population policy gains.

Demographers have been able to argue with some effectiveness that less restrictive divorce laws are anti-natalist influences. I don't believe this anti-natalist effect has been "proved", but at least common sense tells us that if couples can part ways, fertility will decline. I am in favor of the eased divorce laws in part because it just didn't make any sense to have people in the State of New York not being able to get a divorce unless they were rich enough to go to Alabama or Nevada.

I am willing to change many laws which have a pro-natalist influence because I think it makes good sense to change these laws irrespective of their effect on fertility. There are many pro-natalist laws which I am unwilling to change because it does not make good sense to change those laws. I think you have to look at them one by one rather than trying to deal with them as a totality.

Now the other thing that Dr. Tietze took me to task on is the ability of the demographer to make predictions. I believe that he stated that he was willing to live with a 6 percent error in the present world population. Well, I think that's fair enough. I think demographers probably can come within 6 percent. When you make future predictions you are carrying that six percent error all the way through so that you are constantly magnifying the six percent error.

Not much is gained by arguing over the accuracy of estimates of existing world population. Chris Tietze struck at the gut issue which I think attorneys must confront when he urged us to use the prudent man rule in formulating population policy. We attorneys who have dealt with trusts and estates in Massachusetts for years know about the prudent man rule. The only difference is that when you are dealing with certain basic human values you don't apply the same kind of decision making processes that you apply when you are managing a trust or an estate.

Sometimes we lawyers forget that. We forget that there is a difference between manipulating the economy and manipulating a person's basic feelings toward his family and toward his children.

In this discussion, even with Professor Coale, whom I don't accuse of being a hardhearted man, I detected analogies between the way we handle the economy and the way we handle a very basic part of human existence. I see a difference and I think we ought to address ourselves to that difference.

If the figures are as gloomy as a person like Paul Ehrlich seems to think they are, if we honestly believe that disaster is going to follow a failure to arrest the alarmingly high rates of growth in certain underdeveloped countries, I, as a prudent population planner, would not only sanction infanticide, I would seriously consider sanctioning the taking of human life, all people over 65, for example. If we are faced with disaster, like Mr. Holmes in that lifeboat in the middle of the ocean, who, in order to save the remaining people, had to toss overboard some of the passengers, then we must take very firm action. That's what the prudent man would do. That's what Mr. Holmes did when he was in that lifeboat in the middle of the ocean.

I suggest that there is no one on this panel, and I doubt if there is anyone here in this room, who is willing to apply that kind of a prudent man rule even though he foresees disaster, because underneath it he must be hoping for something else. He must be hoping against hope that something is going to happen, because if that thing is not going to happen even the modest kinds of approaches that Professor Tietze is mentioning, or Mr. Gille has mentioned, will not work.

Now I want to deal with what I consider to be a fundamental problem in dealing with the underdeveloped nations because I think that we are pretty much in agreement on what's happening here in the United States.

Everyone seems to agree that population growth in underdeveloped nations is very alarming. In Latin America particularly, and in some parts of Africa, strong pro-natalist laws have greatly inhibited voluntary family planning. Also, many of these nations have not yet begun to devote substantial resources to voluntary family planning.

Before trying to implement stronger fertility control measures, a greater effort should be made to bring to these nations a full panoply of family planning services, accompanied by an effective educational program. Admittedly, such a program would have to be quite imaginative to be effective in nations with a high illiteracy rate and a natural pro-natalistic tendency arising from an agricultural background where children were a basic form of wealth.

I am optimistic that such a program will work because I really can't face what would happen if it does not work. If voluntary family planning, including abortion, does not work, it would be living in a fool's paradise to think some kinds of modest economic incentives are going to work. I have not discovered an example that suggests it is possible to achieve a rapid reduction in fertility, counter to the normal desires of the people involved, by the use of economic incentives. If people want to have children, which they see as a positive value in their life, even the threat of denying them a benefit here or giving them a transistor radio there will not materially affect their fertility patterns. I don't want to make a big issue out of this offer of transistor radios because, as I understand, none were ever given, but the mere thought that somebody would suggest this, however, I do find very terrifying.

The ancient Romans tried to encourage fertility by denying the ability to dispose of property unless one had natural children, but this inducement was unavailing. The Western European countries and Canada, which have family allowance programs, have some of the lowest reproduction rates in the world. Thus, there's no evidence that you can increase the number of children by the use of economic incentives and I have seen no evidence at all that one can decrease fertility by such methods. Having no evidence that economic incentives, which are bound to be detrimental to the poor, are going to work, I would be reluctant to use them.

Dr. Coale

I think you're posing a lot of false dilemmas by insisting that we either do one or the other. Any serious proposal for programs in the underdeveloped countries includes the development of an effective network of family planning facilities and education, including both courses in schools and a whole paraphernalia developed for adult education, from puppet shows to movies.

One of the difficulties in underdeveloped countries is that none of those programs work well and neither does the program of raising agricultural production. The ten percent of the Indian population that is so-to-speak covered by these programs has not reduced its fertility even to what that country would require. It's not true that ten percent has achieved low fertility. Ten percent of the population is within reach of some kind of family planning service, but most of this small percentage does not utilize the service.

Because all programs work badly and underdevelopment leads to further underdevelopment, serious people and not fanatics have proposed incentives. Incidentally, I am not very enthusiastic about them, but I don't oppose them out of hand. They are proposed as part of the whole battery of methods that need to be tried in a difficult situation to try to bring the birth rate down.

This does not mean incentives instead of family planning, but in addition to family planning and to education.

There is a cultural lag in realizing the reduction in mortality so that people who already have six children are not deciding to avoid the seventh, even though none of the six have died. We want to persuade them in every way possible simply because there is, I think, a greater appreciation on the part of people who have examined the whole situation about the seriousness of continued high fertility than there is yet in the minds of the mass of the population.

Even in the long run when everyone is having -- every couple is having the number of children that they want, there should be effort to influence them to have the number that would be more consonant with the overall social norm. I don't mean that we should have a rule that everyone should have a limit of two children. I myself am in favor of encouraging diversity. I would like to see families that range from no children for people who prefer to have none, to one child for people who prefer the one-child family, to five or six, or more. But the average should be about 2.1 in the long run and we should affect the marginal decisions so that the average would work out that way.

Someone who prefers children to color TV sets should be able to have them, but if the birth rate is too high, the choice should be made a little more expensive. I don't think that is coercive; rather, it leaves a maximum of freedom of choice.

Dr. Tietze

Professor Berman has pointed out correctly that some proposed measures of economic deterrents to child bearing, such as abolition of income tax exemption after the second child, would fall heavily on middle income people because the lowest income group does not pay the income tax. Don't you think that it is within the ingenuity of the lawyers to devise a deterrent that falls with relatively equal severity on persons with incomes of $50,000 and $2,000, respectively?

Professor Berman

The only way I can see doing it with the income tax would be to try to make the dependency exemptions decrease with each child; in other words, for the people in the lowest income group you would have a $1,200 dependency exemption for the first child and then $1,000 for the second, $600 for the third and then $400 for succeeding children. Then you would try to make the size of the exemptions inversely proportional to the income, so that a person who was in the 50 percent tax bracket would get a $600 exemption rather than $1200 for the first child, $400 for the second child and then perhaps no exemptions at all beyond the second.

Now if you work that out with the existing demographic data and the statistics for income in the United States, you can probably work it out so that you won't have any real revenue lost while building greater progressivity in the income tax system.

I have seen absolutely no evidence that welfare mothers have additional children when welfare payments are geared to the number of children involved. Almost all of the evidence I have seen is that welfare mothers have the additional children more out of ignorance. The statistics I have seen on the desired family size of the poor are not that different from the desired family size of the affluent. And most welfare departments allow welfare benefits up to four or five children, so that there is almost no evidence I have seen to indicate that people are having children in order to claim additional welfare.

Dr. Coale

I think that's true and that in fact the incidence of unwanted children in low income, low education categories is due either to a contraceptive failure or failure to use contraception for reasons other than wanting immediate birth, the parents not wanting another child at the time the pregnancy occurred or later. Unwanted children, according to the testimony of the mother herself after the child was born, include 66 percent of the fifth or later children, among low income blacks. If we eliminated unwanted children, it would have an effect completely out of line with any effects of welfare payment. It is only a comfortable upper class myth that if these poor people would stop having more children in order to get more welfare, the problem would go away.

Dr. Tietze

I fully agree with what Professor Coale said about the welfare family. However, it has been said, and I think correctly so, that if there is a problem in the United States associated with too rapid population growth, it is due to the fact that the great mass of couples who are not on welfare want families which are too large in terms of what would be most advantageous to the family and advantageous to the community.

Discussion of income tax reform and so forth should not be limited to reduction of deductions before the tax rate is applied. There are many other ways in which you can vary the tax burden. I would think it would be possible to compute the tax on the full income and then allow exemptions on the basis of the number of children, which of course would fall more heavily on the higher income group.

I don't think it would make a great deal of difference one way or the other. I think that even with high taxes this is a relatively minor factor when it comes to the getting of children. Far more important would be the creation of socially acceptable alternative roles for women. It's very hard for a woman with a profession to stay childless when all her friends are having cute little babies. Would the type of social engineering which would promote the creation and social acceptance of such alternative roles for women and for men, too, fall under the type of manipulation which you consider improper?

Professor Berman

Absolutely not. I think one of the most favorable antinatalist things going is women's liberation and I would hope that all you who are lawyers and partners in law firms, would not discriminate in either the hiring or the promotion of women as attorneys in law firms. If that were done and if the academic profession would take a similar attitude, I think we would go a long way towards reducing the birth rate.

Chairman Fox

I think that we will now solicit comments and questions from the audience.

Mrs. Harriet Pilpel

Well, I first want to say that I thoroughly subscribe to Professor Berman's paper, which I think is a very significant contribution, and to its conclusions. But I am disturbed in general by the fact that no member of the panel, including Professor Berman, has really looked at what I would call the micro-side of this problem.

I think it's fun to speculate about incentives and disincentives, but it would also be productive, especially since this is a group of lawyers, to look at the laws that we have even in the United States. Without speculating about the status of women or anything else further removed from the actual problem of fertility, we might review what we are doing to prevent people from exercising freedom of choice by the instrumentality of law.

We have heard discussion this evening about how we don't want to interfere with basic human rights by requiring people not to have children. But we are today and have for decades been interfering with basic human rights by forcing people to have children.

For example, there are only four states where abortion is available except in very restricted circumstances. Very little is being done by the legal profession about that. The abortion reform and repeal movement in this country has not been noted for the participation of lawyers.

In the realm of voluntary sterilization, which has been barely mentioned here this evening, lawyers have done practically nothing. And although we have 100,000 voluntary sterilizations a year in this country, they are obtained at enormous costs in terms of money, in terms of struggle with the authorities. In New York, the Attorney General has ruled the Medicaid funds are not available for voluntary sterilization. Also, voluntary sterilization is not available at most hospitals.

In the contraceptive field, we have even more barriers. We make access to contraception on the part of minors virtually impossible. We have laws against advertising and display of contraceptives.

We have all kinds of complicated rules about referral from one state to another so that doctors are afraid to refer people to New York for abortions. We don't have information readily available and so forth, and so on. It seems to me that one of the first jobs for lawyers ought to be elimination of the myriad such laws which are now on our books.

I'd like to make one more point about marriage. I agree with you that I would not raise the age at which people could get married because that would mean not one-third pregnant brides, presumably, but two-thirds. But I would suggest that serious consideration be given to the proposition that we ought to have two kinds of marriage in this country. Judge Ben Lindsay suggested many years ago that there might be a marriage easy to get into and easy to get out of, which many young people, particularly in the university community, are now living in anyway. Then there would be another kind or marriage, much more difficult to get into and much more difficult to get out of -- Marriage I and Marriage II, or something like that.

In any event, before we even get that theoretical, I suggest that we do not again allow the Congress of the United States to pass a law, which it did last month, prohibiting the dissemination of unsolicited contraceptive information or contraceptives. After almost a hundred years of getting rid of restrictive federal laws, we end up with something which makes any large scale circulation of contraceptives impossible.

I think lawyers have a capacity to adapt themselves to specifics and that's what I hope meetings like this will result in.

Professor Berman

I've always been a little frightened that if voluntary sterilization is readily available, there will then come the economic incentive given to poor persons to engage in voluntary sterilization. If we are careful perhaps we can avoid unfairness and I definitely favor changing laws relating to Medicaid payments, Blue Cross, Blue Shield payments for voluntary sterilization.

Where the demographer and the lawyer have the most difficult time getting together is on this question of dealing with the wanted pregnancy. In other words, how do we change people's desires as to the number of children that they want? To me that is the ultimately more troubling problem because I don't see how to solve that one.

Mr. Frank Patton

Would you think that the rhetoric that Dr. Ehrlich is using in describing the population problem as a crisis is doing a service? Does it create a climate in which we are more apt to be able to adopt laws that are going to be useful in solving the problem?

Professor Coale

It's an embarrassing question for me to answer because I recently wrote a rather unfavorable review of Dr. Ehrlich's book. I think the reason my answer is complex is that Ehrlich and the others who write in that vein have probably performed some kind of service for the country by calling dramatic attention to the problems of environmental deterioration and

-61-

pollution and so on.   But I am wary about whether it really in the long run performs a service to resort to what I think is crisis-mongering.

An example, in extreme form, was provided by the Paddock brothers, who wrote a book called Famine 1975. Since we are not going to have any famines between now and 1975, my reaction is that a lot of people will think that the problem is not very bad.

They have painted the picture of running out of oxygen and various other consequences which turn out very quickly not to be right.   Although there has been a fever pitch of attention because of the dramatic nature of the statements, my own conservative and sort of scientific bias is that you get along further by dealing strictly with the truth and not by exaggerating.

Mr. Michael Butterworth

There is a seeming inconsistency with your very, very great sensitivity towards coercion implicit in economic incentives, particularly to engage in voluntary sterilization, and your support of widespread and quite readily available abortion.

Professor Berman

As you move up the scale of pregnancy, it seems to me that abortion closely resembles infanticide, which I don't countenance, even though I can think of some very good reasons for having it.   For example, it deals effectively with the sex preference problem.   There are some very good reasons for having infanticide if what you are primarily interested in is population control.   But I'm opposed to infanticide. And when you start performing abortions in the eighth or ninth month of pregnancy, I have a hard time distinguishing between abortion and infanticide.   Also the cases having to determine whether or not a mother is guilty of homicide or guilty of self-induced abortion, present line-drawing problems, some of them drawing at the umbilical cord and so forth. Talking strictly about population control, I would limit abortion to the first trimester of pregnancy, where the mortality rate of the mother is held at a very low rate. But there are non-population control reasons that do lead me to favor something like the New York law which allows abortion on demand further into pregnancy.

-62-

Because I think people ought to have a choice, I would make sterilization freely available, but if we are not careful, it's easy to use sterilization as a permanent form of population control and the people who would respond to that would in fact be the poor.

Professor Coale

I think there is a distinction between penalties and rewards.

I am not a strong advocate of this, but I think the position shouldn't be undersold just the same. Let me take the concrete case of withholding welfare benefits. Now actually the purpose of welfare benefits is not pro-natalist. It's to provide for the welfare of the child. Actually, that's also true of income tax exemptions, which are not intended to be pro-natalist, but are supposed to equalize the economic circumstances of families of different sizes. I would be opposed to withholding welfare for the child because it would immediately be to his disadvantage and its effect on the fertility of the mother would be indirect. On the other hand, the kind of incentive proposal difficult to administer, that economists have made, is that a married couple is given an annual payment for every year in which the woman doesn't get pregnant.

This positive inducement not to get pregnant does not operate to the disadvantage of a poor child who doesn't get his welfare payment. I don't think it's true that benefits are exactly the same thing as penalties. They redistribute income, but to say they are the same thing obscures the issue.

Dr. Tietze

May I put this on a somewhat pointed basis. Isn't it true that a penalty is a withholding of a benefit to which you have become used, rather than the other way around?

Professor Berman

I'd just like to answer one thing with Professor Coale about the proposal of rewarding mothers for not having children.

It is true that when one analyzes just that transaction it doesn't seem to be coercive. My only objection to it is that if we are going to spend public funds, we are making choices, and what we are doing is we are making the choice to reward the person who engages in the anti-natalist policy.

We could equally take that thousand dollars and give it to the poor family living in Harlem in order to get better housing.

In other words, we always have to make choices when we are talking about resource allocation. And I would, at this stage of our development, if given those kinds of choices in the United States, I would clearly make them in favor of some kind of increased guaranteed annual income rather than rewarding the mother who doesn't have children.

Mr. Walter Bokdar

It seems to me that you all have not mentioned a factor I think that bears very closely on the population problem, and that is the ecological and psychological effects of overpopulation.

One example in the paper today projects power needs for the next thirty or forty years, which based on present population would necessitate massive air and water pollution, or thermal pollution. Just to cope with the population if we had ZPG today will require almost devasting effects upon aspects of our environment and on what we call the quality of life.

Professor Coale

It would take me too long to go into it very extensively, but let me say that I share your concern about the environment. However, I feel that population has been a mistaken target in looking for the place to put the blame. What seems to me to be the predominant factor in causing the deterioriation of our environment has been our total neglect of it. Our market economy--and the same thing is true in Russia--favors the production of consumer goods, without penalizing for producing detrimental consequences. For example, Con Edison gets money for selling us electricity and until very recently was not penalized for deteriorating our environment.

We have treated water and air as if they were free. In the modern industrial society we can't.

I think we would have many of the same environmental

problems if our population were only half as big. They have them in Australia. I think that's the clearest case. Sydney has pollution and traffic problems, and so on. Australia has 11 or 12 million people in an area almost as big as the United States.

It's also true that the pollution problems are not substantially worse and in many instances not as bad in countries like England, whose population density is ten times ours. They have cleaned up pollution now out of the air in London to a great extent. They have also cleaned out the San Diego Bay even though San Diego continues to burgeon. I think one can handle these problems by paying attention to them and paying the cost and making people clean up their trash and so on. If we don't do those things, we are headed for an environmental catastrophe, and if we do do it, why the fact that our population is bound to go up another thirty percent won't make a lot of difference.

S. William Green

I was struck by Professor Berman's comment that instead of giving a thousand dollars for each year of non-pregnancy to a woman, he'd rather use that resource to give better housing in Harlem, and I was particularly struck by it because I am regional administrator for the U. S. Department of Housing and Urban Development.

Then I started to do a little calculating. It costs approximately something around $4,000 to create an extra bedroom on a public housing project in New York City. I don't know what the exact cost per year for educating a child in New York City public schools is but I imagine it is running about a thousand dollars per year per child.

Might not there be an economy which would actually leave more resources to deal with social problems given the fact we had a modest incentive for not creating more children?

Professor Berman

What you are saying is that perhaps in the long run, if we could pay people not to have children, you may be able to in effect achieve a better life for everybody, those people in Harlem and those people at Sutton Place. I take it this problem is much greater where your child dependency costs just drain off tremendous amounts of your societal resources. My only answer is that the United States has the capacity to do both. I am afraid that as a practical matter you are talking about a tradeoff. In other words, we are not going to increase our taxes and pay for the housing in Harlem and for these additional payments not to have children. In the underdeveloped nations of the world, you may have no choice.

Professor Coale

I think we could address that problem much more directly by making more effective birth control available to the inhabitants of Harlem, so that the 66 percent of the higher order children that are unwanted are not born, simply by making services available to them now. I don't think the incentive plan is so badly needed.

Chairman Fox

Out of respect to our distinguished guests, although many of us would like to continue this fascinating program, I think we had better terminate it. I believe that this will be a significant addition to the honorable history of the Hammarskjöld Forums, and we are very grateful to you, Professor Coale, Dr. Tietze, Professor Berman, Mr. Gille, and Dr. Viel.

Bibliography

Selected Bibliography on

Population Policy

Prepared by Anthony P. Grech
Librarian, The Association of the Bar
of the City of New York

REFERENCES

Association of the Bar of the City of New York. Library. Legal
aspects of abortion (bibliography). 1967. 22 Record 118-23.
Bibliography on population. Aug. 1966. 22 Poplt'n Bull. 20p.
ref. supp.
California State Library. Law Library. A selective biblio-
graphy on population control--abortion, birth control, eutha-
nasia and sterilization. March 1966. Sacramento. 1966.
16p.
Population Council, New York.
International institute for the study of human reproduction.
Reports on population. New York. Oct. 1969--.
Studies in family planning. No. 1--. New York. June 1963--.
Population index volume 1--. 1935--. Princeton, Off. of Popu-
lation Research, Princeton University and the Population
Association of America. (quarterly)
Population Reference Bureau, Inc. People, vol. 1--, no. 1--.
May 1970--.
Smith, Solomon C. Bibliography: abortion--selected recent
writings. New Haven, Yale Law Library. 1969? 6p.
A sourcebook of population. Nov. 1969. 25 Poplt'n Bull. 1-51.
Texas University. Population Research Center. International
population census bibliography. Austin, Bureau of Bus. Res.,
University of Texas. 1965--.

Tietze, Christopher. Bibliography of fertility control: 1950-1965. New York, National Committee on Maternal Health. 1965.

United Nations. Statistical Office.
Demographic yearbook; annuaire démographique. 1948--. (annual)
Population and vital statistics reports. Vol. 1--.

U.S. Bureau of the Census. International population reports. Series P-90, no. 1--. Washington, Gov't Print. Off. 1952--.

OFFICIAL AND DOCUMENTARY SOURCES

Problems of population growth; message from President Nixon to congress. 1969. 61 Dep't State Bull. 105-11.

United Nations. Asian Population Conference, New Delhi, India, 1963. Report...and selected papers. New York. 1964. 207p. (E/CN.11/670)

United Nations. Commission for Asia and the Far East. Working group on administrative aspects of family planning programmes. Report. New York. 1966. 64p. (E/CN.11/742)

United Nations. Dep't of Economic and Social Affairs.
The concept of a stable population: applications to the study of populations of countries with incomplete demographic statistics. 1969. 237p.
The determinants and consequences of population trends. A summary of findings of studies of interrelationships of demographic, economic and social factors based on a world-wide survey of scientific literature. 1953. 404p.
Population newsletter. No. 1--. 1968--.

United Nations. Economic and Social Council. Report of the population commission. World population situation. Report of the secretary-general, 30 Jan. 1970. 29p. (E/4778. CE/CN.9/231/Summary/Rev. 1)

United Nations. Population bulletin no. 7--1963. With special reference to conditions and trends of fertility. New York. 1964. 151p. (64.XIII)

United Nations. Population Commission. World population situation, 23 Sept. 1969. 206p. (E/CN.9/231) (mimeo)

U.N. report on the world social situation. 1967.

United Nations. Secretariat. Findings of studies on the relationship between population trends and economic and social factors; report. Lake Success. 1950. 170p. (UN Doc. E/CN.9/55/11 April 1950)

United Nations. Statistical Office,
   Demographic yearbook; annuaire démographique. 1948--.
   (annual)
   Population and vital statistics reports vol. 1--. Jan. 1949--.
   New York.
U.S. Agency for International Development. Bureau for Techni-
   cal Assistance. Office of Population. Population program
   assistance: aid to developing nations by the United States,
   other nations, and international and private agencies, Oct.
   1969. Washington. 1969. 163p.
U.S. Congress. House. Message from president of the United
   States relative to population growth, July 21, 1969. 9p.
   (House doc. 139, 91st cong.)
U.S. Congress. House. Comm. on Agriculture (89.2). World
   war on hunger: staff summary of testimony presented by public witnesses at hearings on world food and population problems Feb. 14-18, 1966. Washington, Gov't Print. Off. 1966.
   19p.
U.S. Congress. House. Comm. on Government Operations.
   (91.1) Commission on population growth and American future,
   report...to accompany H.R. 15165. Washington, Gov't Print.
   Off. 1969. 19p.
   (91.1) Effects of population growth on natural resources and
   the environment. Hearings before a subcom...Sept. 15 and
   16, 1969. Washington, Gov't Print. Off. 1969. 256p.
   (91.1) Establishing a commission on population growth and
   related matters, hearings...on S.2701 and related house bills,
   Nov. 19 and 20, 1970. Washington, Gov't Print. Off. 1970.
   102p.
U.S. Congress. Senate. Comm. on Government Operations.
   (91.1) Establish commission on population growth and
   American future. Hearings...on S.2701, Sept. 15, 1969.
   Washington, Gov't Print. Off. 1969. 244p.
   (91.1) Establish commission on population growth and
   American future. Report...to accompany S.2701, Sept. 24,
   1969. Washington, Gov't Print. Off. 1969. 10p.
U.S. Congress. Senate. Comm. on Government Operations.
   Subcom. on Foreign Aid Expenditures.
   (89.1) Population crisis: hearings, June 22, 23, Aug. 24,
   25, 31-Sept. 22, 1966 on S.1676, a bill to reorganize the department of health, education & welfare...Washington, Gov't
   Print. Off. 1966. 4 pts.
   (90.1/2) Population crisis: hearings, pts. 1-2, Nov. 2, 1967-

Jan. 31, 1968; pt. 3, Feb. 1, 1968; pt. 4, index on S.1676, a bill to reorganize the department of state and the department of health, education & welfare. Washington, Gov't Print. Off. 1967-68. 4pts.

U.S. Congress. Senate. Comm. on Labor and Public Welfare. (91.1/2) Family planning and population research, 1970: hearings, Dec. 8, 1969-Feb. 19, 1970, on S.2108, to promote public health and welfare by expanding, improving and better coordinating the family planning services and population research activities of the federal government, and for other purposes; S.3219, to amend the public health service act to training and technical assistance. Washington, Gov't Print. Off. 1970. 541p.

(91.2) Expanding, improving and better coordinating family planning services and population research activities of federal government. Report...to accompany S.2108, July 7, 1970. Washington, Gov't Print. Off. 1970. 21p.

U.S. Federal Council for Science and Technology. Ad Hoc Group on Population Research. The federal program in population research; report to the federal council for science and technology. Washington, Executive office of the President, Off. of Science and Technology. Gov't Print. Off. 1969. 115p.

U.S. International Development Agency
Population challenge, U.S. aid and family planning in less-developed countries. Washington, Gov't Print. Off. 1968. 20p.

Population program assistance, aid to developing nations by United States, other nations and international and private agencies, prepared by office of population, bureau of technical assistance, A.I.D. Washington, Gov't Print. Off. 1969. 163p.

United States President's Commission on Population and Family Planning. Population and family planning: the transition from concern to action. Wilbur J. Cohen, chairman. Washington. 1968. 43p.

World Population Conference, 2d, Belgrade, 1965. Proceedings. New York, United Nations. 1966. (U.N. Doc. E/Conf. 41/2)

BOOKS AND PAMPHLETS

American Academy of Political and Social Science, Philadelphia. World population. Edited by John D. Durand. Philadelphia. 1967. 254p.

American Assembly.

    Overcoming world hunger. Clifford M. Hardin, ed. Englewood Cliffs, N.J., Prentice-Hall. 1969. 177p.

    The population dilemma. 2d ed. Philip M. Hauser, ed. Englewood Cliffs, N.J., Prentice-Hall. 1969. 211p.

American Public Health Association. Program Comm. on Population and Public Health. Family planning: a guide for state and local agencies. New York. 1968. 154p.

Berelson, Bernard. Family-planning programs; an international survey. New York, Basic Books. 1969. 310p.

Black, Eugene R.

    Population increase and economic development (In Young, L.B., ed. Population in perspective. N.Y., Oxford univ. press, 1968, pp. 132-35)

    Population increase and economic development (In Osborn, Fairfield, ed. Our crowded planet. Garden City, Doubleday, 1962, pp. 83-91)

Bogue, Donald J., ed. Mass communication and motivation for birth control; proceedings of the summer workshops at the University of Chicago. Chicago. 1967. 551p.

Borrie, Wilfred David. The growth and control of world population. London, Weidenfeld & Nicolson. 1970. 340p.

Bourgeois-Pichat, Jean. Population growth and development. New York, Carnegie Endowment for International Peace. 1966. 81p. (Int'l conciliation no. 556)

Bouthone, G. La surpopulation; l'inflation démographique. Paris, Payot. 1964. 250p.

Brayer, Franklin T., ed. World population and U.S. government policy and programs. Washington, George Washington Univ. Press. 1968. 116p.

Callahan, Daniel, ed. The Catholic case for contraception. London, Macmillan. 1969. 240p.

Carr-Saunders, Alexander Morris (Sir). World population, past growth and present trends. New York, Barnes & Noble. 1965. 336p.

Chamberlain, Neil W. Beyond Malthus; population and power. New York, Basic Books. 1970. 214p.

Chicago. University. Norman Wait Harris Memorial Foundation. 30th Institute 1954. Population and world politics, edited by Philip M. Hauser. Bombay, Jaico Pub. House. 1968. 316p.

Clark, Colin. Population growth and land use. London, Melbourne, Macmillan; New York, St. Martin's Press. 1967. 406p.

Clark, Grenville.
Disarmament and the population problem (In Larson, A., ed., A warless world. N.Y., McGraw-Hill, 1963, pp.88-97)
Population pressures and peace (In Osborn, Fairfield, ed. Our crowded planet. Garden City, Doubleday, 1962, pp. 123-33)

Coale, Ansley J. Effect of density (In Young, L.B., ed. Population in perspective. N.Y., Oxford univ. press, 1968, pp. 135-49)

Coale, Ansley J. and Hoover, Edgar M. Population growth and economic development in low income countries; a case study of India's prospects. Princeton, Princeton Univ. Press. 1958. 389p.

Commager, Henry Steele. Overpopulation and the new nations (In Osborn, Fairfield, ed. Our crowded planet. Garden City, Doubleday, 1962, pp. 117-21)

Conference on Population, 1st, Princeton, N.J., 1968. Growth of population; consequences and controls. Proceedings...Sept. 27 to 30, 1968. Edited by M.C. Shelesnyak. New York, Gordon and Breach. 1969. 458p.

Conference on Research in Family Planning, New York, 1960. Research in family planning; papers presented at a conference sponsored jointly by the Milbank memorial fund and the Population council, inc. held Oct. 13-19, 1960...edited by Clyde V. Kiser. Princeton, Princeton Univ. Press. 1962. 662p.

Conference on World Population Problems, Indiana University, 1967. World population: the view ahead: proceedings...held at Indiana university, Bloomington, May 3-6, 1967. Bloomington. 1968. 310p.

Conway, Freda. World population trends (In Birmingham, W. and Ford, A.G., eds. Planning and growth in rich and poor countries. London, Allen & Unwin, 1966, pp.250-61)

Corwin, Arthur F. World population and American responsibility. Davis, Dep't of History, University of California. 1968. 75p.

Davis, Kingsley. Population (In Young, L.B., ed. Population in perspective. N.Y., Oxford univ. press. 1968, pp. 116-32)

Day, Lincoln H. and Taylor, Alice. Too many Americans. Boston, Houghton, Mifflin. 1964. 298p.

Ehrlich, Paul R. The population bomb. New York, Ballantine Books. 1968. 223p.

Ehrlich, Paul R. and Ehrlich, A.H. Population, resources, environment; issues in human ecology. San Francisco, W.H. Freeman. 1970. 383p.

Enke, Stephen. Economics for development. Englewood Cliffs, N.J., Prentice-Hall. 1963. 616p.

Family and fertility; proceedings of the fifth Notre Dame conference on population, Dec. 1-3, 1966, edited by William T. Liu. Notre Dame, Notre Dame Univ. Press. 1967. 257p.

Fertility and family planning: a world view. Papers presented at university of Michigan, sesquicentennial celebration, Nov. 1967. (Behrman, S.J.; Corsa, Leslie, jr. and Freedman, Ronald, eds.) Ann Arbor, Univ. of Michigan Press. 1969. 503p.

Fitzgibbon, R.H. Political implications of population growth in Latin America (In Halmos, P., ed. Latin American sociological studies. Keele, University, 1967, pp. 23-45)

Freedman, Ronald. The sociology of human fertility: a trend report and bibliography (In Current sociology X/XI, (2), Oxford, Basil Blackwell, 1963, 121p.)

Gardner, Richard N. Population growth: a world problem; statement of U.S. policy. Washington, Gov't Print. Off. 1963. 16p. (Dep't of State pub. 7485)

af Geijerstam, G.K., ed. An annotated bibliography of induced abortion. Ann Arbor, Univ. of Michigan, Center for Population Planning. 1969. 359p.

Geisert, Harold L. The control of world population growth. Washington, Population Research Project, George Washington University. 1963. 50p.

Gray, H.P., Comp. Economic development and population growth; a conflict? Lexington, Mass. Heath. 1970. 162p.

Hance, William A. Population, migration and urbanization in Africa. New York, Columbia Univ. Press. 1970. 450p.

Hauser, Philip M.
    Population, poverty and world politics. Urbana, Dep't of Political Science, University of Illinois. 1965. 16p.
    World population problems. New York, Foreign Policy Association. 1965. 46p.

Hauser, Philip M. and Duncan, Otis Dudley, eds. The study of population: an inventory and appraisal. Chicago, Univ. of Chicago Press. 1959. 864p.

Heer, David M. Society and population. Englewood Cliffs, N.J., Prentice-Hall. 1968. 118p.

Holler, J.E. Population growth and social change in the middle east. Washington, George Washington University, Population Research Project. 1964. 52p.

Hoselitz, Bert F. and Hargreaves, H.W. Population growth and economic development (In Gallaher, A., jr. Perspectives in developmental change. Lexington, Univ. of Kentucky press, 1968, pp. 101-29)

International Conference on Family Planning Programs, Geneva, 1965. Family planning and population programs, a review of world developments. Chicago, Univ. of Chicago Press. 1966. 848p.

International Conference on Population, Baltimore, 1964. Population dynamics; international action and training programs. Proceedings...May 1964, the Johns Hopkins school of hygiene and public health. Edited by M. Muramatsu and P.A. Harper. Baltimore, Johns Hopkins Press. 1965. 248p.

International Planned Parenthood Federation. Population. Rev. ed. London, International Planned Parenthood Federation. 1969. 17p.

International Planned Parenthood Federation. South East Asia and Oceania Region. Proceedings of the conference...held in Bandung, June 1969. Editors: R.K.B. Hankinson and Nani Soewondo. London. 1969. 260p.

Johnson, Stanley. Life without birth: a journey through the third world in search of the population explosion. London, Heinemann. 1970. 364p.

Jones, Gavin W. The economic effect of declining fertility in less developed countries. 1969. 30p. (Population council, N.Y., Occasional paper)

Kammeyer, Kenneth C.W., comp. Population studies; selected essays and research. Chicago, Rand McNally. 1969. 481p.

King, R.T.F. Population, food supplies and economic growth (In Hutchinson, J., ed. Population and food supply, Cambridge, University press, 1969, pp. 28-47)

Little, A.N. The population problem (In Robinson, R., ed. Overcoming obstacles to economic development; impressions and papers of the fourth Cambridge conference on development problems, 12-25 Sept. 1965 at Jesus college, Cambridge, Cambridge university overseas studio committee, 1966, pp. 62-69)

McCormack, Arthur. The population problem. New York, Crowell. 1970. 264p.

Minnesota-Dakotas Assembly on the Population Dilemma, Moorhead, Minn., 1964. The population dilemma; final report. Minneapolis, Extension Div., University of Minnesota. 1964. 37p.

Mudd, Stuart, ed. The population crisis and the use of world resources. Bloomington, Indiana Univ. Press. 1964. 562p.

Myrdal, Gunnar. Asian drama: an inquiry into the poverty of nations. New York, Twentieth Century Fund. 1968. 3v.

National Academy of Sciences. Comm. on Science and Public Policy.
The growth of world population; analysis of the problems and recommendations for research and training. 1963. 38p. (Nat'l research council pub. 1091)
Growth of U.S. population. Washington. 1965. 25p.

Nevett, A. Population; explosion or control? A study with special reference to India. London, Geoffrey Chapman. 1964. 224p.

Ng, Larry K.Y., ed. The population crisis; implications and plans for action. Bloomington, Indiana Univ. Press. 1965. 364p.

Ohlin, Goran, Population control and economic development. Paris, Development Center of the Organization for Economic Cooperation and Development. 1967. 138p.

Organisation for Economic Co-operation and Development. Development Centre
International assistance for population programmes: recipient and donor views. Paris. 1970. 185p.
Population programmes and economic and social development. Paris. 1970. 141p.

Organski, Katherine and A.F.K. Population and world power. New York, Knopf. 1961. 63p.

Osborn, Fairfield, ed. Our crowded planet: essays on the pressures of population. Garden City, Doubleday. 1962. 240p.

Osborn, Frederick.
Population: an international dilemma. New York, Population Council. 1958.
This crowded world. New York, Public Affairs Committee. 1960. 28p. (Pub. aff. pam. no. 306)
The future of human heredity. New York, Weybright and Talley. 1968.

Petersen, William
The politics of population. New York, Doubleday. 1964. 350p.
Population. 2d ed. New York, Macmillan. 1969. 700p.

Planned Parenthood-World Population Center for Family Planning Program Development. Need for subsidized family planning services: United States, each state and county 1968.

A report...Washington, Gov't Print. Off. 1969. 255p. (OEO pam. 61306)

Population Council, New York. The population council 1952-1964; a report. New York. 1965. 63p.

Population Crisis Committee. Foreign aid for family planning; proposal for action in the congress of the United States. Washington. 1967. 48p.

Population growth and its implications: a bibliography (In Quinn, F.X., ed. Population ethics. Washington, Corpus Books, 1968, pp. 109-40)

The problem of population. Proceedings of the conferences of the university of Notre Dame and the Cana conference of Chicago, 1963-65. Notre Dame Univ. of Notre Dame Press. 1964-65. 3v.

Sauvy, A. Fertility and survival; population problems from Malthus to Mao Tse-tung. New York, Collier Books. 1963. 287p.

Sheps, Mindell C. and Ridley, Jeanne C., eds. Public health and population change. Pittsburgh, Univ. of Pittsburgh Press. 1965. 557p.

Social demography and medical responsibility: proceedings of sixth conference of the International planned parenthood federation, Europe and Near East region, held in Budapest, Sept. 1969. London, International Planned Parenthood Federation. 1970. 168p.

Spengler, Joseph J. and Duncan, Otis Dudley, eds. Population theory and policy: selected readings. Glencoe, Ill., Free Press. 1956. 522p.

Studies in family planning. New York, Population Council, Inc. 1963.

Stycos, J. Mayone.
    Human fertility in Latin America: sociological perspectives. Ithaca, Cornell Univ. Press. 1968. 318p.
    Survey research and population control in Latin America (In Maramatsu, M. and Harper, P.A., eds. Population dynamics--international action and training programs; proceedings of the international conference on population, May 1964, Johns Hopkins school of hygiene and public health. Baltimore, Johns Hopkins univ. press, 1965, pp. 161-67)

Stycos, J. Mayone and Areas, Jorge, eds. Population dilemma in Latin America. Washington, Potomac Books. 1966. 249p.

Symposium on Population Growth: Crisis and Challenge, 1st, Green Bay, Wis., 1970. Population growth...proceedings.

Edited by John H. Beaton and Alexander R. Doberenz. Green Bay, College of Human Biology, University of Wisconsin. 1970. 140p.

Taeuber, Irene B. Policies, programs and the decline of birth rates; China and the Chinese populations of east Asia (In Maramatsu, M. and Harper, P.A., eds., Population dynamics--international action and training programs; proceedings of the international conference on population, May 1964, Johns Hopkins school of hygiene and public health. Baltimore, Johns Hopkins univ. press, 1965, pp. 99-104)

Thompson, Warren S. and Lewis, David T. Population problems. 5th ed. New York, McGraw-Hill. 1965. 593p.

Tietze, Christopher.
Fertility control. 1968. 5 Int'l Encyc. Soc. Sci. 38 -88. Modern methods of contraception: an assessment of the effectiveness, acceptability, and safety (In Rubin, A., ed. Family planning today, Phila., Davis, 1969, pp. 9-28) Population growth and its control: socioeconomic health and philosophic aspects (In Prywes, M. and Davies, A.M., eds. Health problems in developing states. N.Y., Grune & Stratton, 1968, pp. 183-90) Also in 4 Israel J. Med. Sci. 503-10.

United Nations Association of the United States of America. National policy panel on world population. World population: a challenge to the United Nations and its system of agencies. 1969. 58p.

Viel, Benjamin. La explosión demográfica ¿cuántos son demasiados? Santiago, Universidad de Chile. 1966. 241p.

Weinberg, Roy D. Laws governing family planning. Dobbs Ferry, N.Y., Oceana. 1968. 118p.

Whelton, Pascal K.; Campbell, Arthur A. and Patterson, John E. Fertility and family planning in the United States. Princeton, Princeton Univ. Press. 1966. 443p.

World leaders declaration on population, presented at the United Nations on human rights day, Dec. 1967. New York, Population Council. 1968. 15p.

World views of population problems. Edited by E. Szabady (and others). Budapest, Akádemiai Kiadó. 1968. 447p.

Young, Louise B., ed. Population in perspective. New York, London, Oxford Univ. Press. 1968. 460p.

PERIODICAL REFERENCES

Ackerman, Edward A. Population, natural resources and technology. 1967. 369 Annals 84-97.

American attitudes on population policy: recent trends. May 1968. 30 Stud. in Family Plan. 1-7.

Back, Kurt W. and Winsborough, Halliman H. Population policy: opinions and actions of governments. 1968/69. 32 (4) Pub. Opinion Q. 634-45.

Baker, Ronald M. Population control in the year 2000--the constitutionality of placing anti-fertility agents in the water supply. 1971. 32 Ohio S. L. J. 108-18.

Baudot, J. and Hugres, P. d'. La conférence démographique européenne. Strasbourg, 30 août-6 septembre 1966. Jan/Feb. 1967. 22 Population (France) 9-80.

Berelson, Bernard.
Beyond family planning. Feb. 1969. 38 Stud. in Family Plan. 1-16.

National family planning programs: where we stand. March 1969. 39 Stud. in Family Plan. (supp.) 341-87.

The present state of family planning programs. Sept. 1970. 57 Stud. in Family Plan. 1-11.

Blake, Judith. Population policy for Americans: is the government being misled? 1969. 164 Science 522-29.

Blaustein, Albert. Arguendo: the legal challenge of population control. 1968. 3 Law & Soc'y Rev. 107-14.

Bogue, Donald J. Prospects for population control. 1967. 49 J. Farm Econ. 1094-97.

Bower, Leonard. The return from investment in population control in less developed countries. 1968. 5 (1) Demography 422-32.

Chandrasekhar, S. How India is tackling her population problem. Oct. 1968. 47 For. Aff. 139-50.

Chen Pi-chao. The political economics of population growth: the case of China. 1971. 23 World Pol. 245-72.

Clark, C. World power and population. May 20, 1969. 21 Nat'l Rev. 481-84.

Clark, Homer H., jr. Law as an instrument of population control. 1968. 40 U. Colo. L. Rev. 179-98.

Claxton, P.P., jr.
Population and law. 1971. 5 Int'l Law. 1.

United States population policy, origins and development: address Aug. 21, 1970. Sept. 21, 1970. 63 Dep't State Bull. 317-26.

Coale, Ansley J. Should the United States start a campaign for fewer births? 1968. 34 (4) Poplt'n Index 467-74.

Cook, Robert C.
Soviet population theory from Marx to Kosygin; a demographic turning point? Oct. 1967. 23 Poplt'n Bull. 85-115.
The world bank tackles population. Nov. 1968. 24 Poplt'n Bull. 57-68.
World population growth. 1960. 25 Law & Contemp. Prob. 379-88.
World population prospects. 1966. 27 Ohio St. L.J. 634-46.

Curtin, T.R.C. The economics of population growth and control in developing countries. 1969. 27 (2) Rev. Soc. Economy 139-53; 1970. 28 (1): 101-05.

Davis, Kingsley. La situación de América Latina en la historia demográfica mundial. Abril/Junho 1964. 7 América Latina 15-44.

Draper, William H., jr. Zero population growth by the year 2000? April 1970. 10 War/Peace Rep. 16-17.

Driver, Edwin D. Population policies of state governments in the United States: some preliminary observations. 1970. 15 Vill. L. Rev. 818-53.

Dumont, René. Surpeuplement chinois et ses conséquences. 1965. 30 (6) Politique Etrangère 486-97.

Durand, John D. A long-range view of world population growth. 1967. 369 Annals 1-8.

Easterlin, Richard A. Effects of population growth on the economic development of developing countries. 1967. 369 Annals 98-120.

Egeberg, Roger O. Defusing the population bomb: new role for government? Aug/Sept. 1970. 6 Trial 10-11.

Eldridge, Hope Tisdale. Population policies. 1968. 12 Int'l Encyc. Soc. Sci. 381 88.

Elkins, Bettye S. Constitutional problems of population control. 1970. 4 J. Law Reform 63-84.

Enke, Stephen. The economic aspects of slowing population growth. March 1966. 76 Econ. J. 44-56.

Fagley, Richard M. A Protestant view of population control. 1960. 25 Law & Contemp. Prob. 470-98.

Falk, Richard A. World population and international law. 1969. 63 Am. J. Int'l L. 514-20.

Feierabend, Ivo K. and Rosalind L. Aggressive behaviors within polities, 1948-1962: a cross-national study. 1966. 10 J. Conflict Resolution 249-71.

Gallagher, Charles F. The United Nations system and population problems. April 1970. 13p. (Fieldstaff reps. West Europe ser. v. 5, no.5)

Gardner, Richard N.

New tasks for the 70's: we are awakening to the realization that all mankind depends on the same scarce and relatively shrinking resource pool. May/June 1970. 5 Vista 29.

Quality of life; a proposed program for global action by the U.N. 1970. 36 Vital Speeches 466-70.

Toward a world population program. 1968. 22 Int'l Org. 332-61.

Garlot, E. Activité des organisations internationales en matière démographique (à suivre). 1969. 24 Population (France) 757-80.

Gonzalez, Alfonso. Some effects of population growth on Latin America's economy. 1967. 9 J. Inter-Am. Stud. 22-42.

Government seeks ways to limit population growth. June 12, 1970. 28 Cong. Q. Weekly Rep. 1554-58.

Groenman, S. The first European population conference. Nov. 1966. Migration Today 31-33.

Guzevaty, Y. Population and world politics. Oct. 1967. Int'l Aff. (Moscow) 59-64.

Hanley, Dexter L. The Catholic and population policy. 1966. 12 Catholic Law. 330-37, 353.

Harkavy, Oscar et al. Family planning and public policy: who is misleading whom? 1969. 165 Science 367-73.

Hauser, Philip M.

Man and more men: the population prospects. June 1964. 20 Bull. Atomic Sci. 41-8.

On population and environment--address. 1970. 36 Vital Speeches 696-701.

Hurewitz, J.C. Politics of rapid population growth in the middle east. 1965. 19 (1) J. Int'l Aff. 26-38.

Jaffe, Frederick S. Family planning, public policy and intervention strategy. 1967. 23 (4) J. Soc. Issues 145-63.

Kamerschen, David R.

Four fallacies regarding the population situation in underdeveloped countries. Feb. 1967. 9 Asian Econ. Rev. 145-85.

Population policies in underdeveloped countries. March 1968.

Katz, Michael. Legal dimensions of population policy. 1969. 50 (3) Soc. Sci. Q. 731-41.

Kellogg, Alfred C. Population growth and international law. 1970. 3 Cornell Int'l L.J. 93-103.

Keyfitz, N. Population and society. 1969. 24 Int'l J. 426-48.

Kirk, Dudley. Prospects for reducing natality in the underdeveloped world. 1967. 369 Annals 48-60.

Kirk, Dudley and Nortman, D. Population policies in developing countries. 1967. 15 Econ. Devel. & Cultural Change 129-42.

Krotki, Karol J. Prospects for population control. 1967. 49 J. Farm Econ. 1098-1105. (Critique of the article by Donald J. Bogue, pp. 1094-97)

Lui, Alfred B. Population growth and education development. 1967. 369 Annals 109-20.

Mayer, Jean. Toward a non-Malthusian population policy. July 1969. 47 (3, pt.2) Milbank Mem'l Fund Q. 340-53; also in Colum. Forum, Summer 1969, pp. 5-13.

Meade, J.E. Population explosion, the standard of living and social conflict. 1967. 77 Econ. J. 233-55.

Means, Cyril C. The constitutional aspects of a national population policy. 1970. 15 Vill. L. Rev. 854-62.

Miro, Carmen A. The world population; two distinct "blocs." Summer 1966. 1 Latin Amer. Res. Rev. 5-16.

Moore, Marvin M. Legal action to stop our population explosion. 1963. 12 Clev.-Mar. L. Rev. 314-29.

Muhsam, H.V. Sur les relations entre la croissance de la population et le développement économique. 1970. 25 Population (France) 347-62.

Narayanan, R. Population control as an aspect of United States policy. 1968. 10 Int'l Stud. 131-62.

National population programs and policy: social and legal implications (Donald A. Gianella, Carl S. Shultz, H. Y. Tien, Samuel M. Wishik, Edwin D. Driver and Cyril C. Means, jr.). 1970. 15 Vill. L. Rev. 785-886.

Notestein, Frank W.
    The population crisis: reasons for hope. 1967. 46 For. Aff. 167-80.
    Zero population growth: what is it? 1970. 2 (2) Family Plan. Perspectives 20-24.

Paillat, Paul. Les perspectives démographiques des pays sous-développés. 1968. 24 Rev. de Défense Nationale 1025-33.

Perkin, Gordon W. Population policy and programmes in southeast Asia: a discussion of limiting factors. 1969. 4 (3) Advances in Fertility Control 37-42.

Peter, Alexander M. The brave new world: can the law bring order within traditional concepts of due process? 1970. 4 Suffolk U.L. Rev. 894-919.

Population Association of America. Progress and problems of fertility control around the world. 1968. 5 (2) Demography 539-1001.

Revelle, Roger. International cooperation in food and population. Winter 1968. 22 Int'l Org. 363-91

St. John-Stevas, Norman. A Roman Catholic view of population control. 1960. 25 Law & Contemp. Prob. 445-69.

Schnore, Leo F. Demography and human ecology: some apparent trends. 1970. 390 Annals 120-28.

Sharma, P.M. Power-politics and population. Jan/Feb. 1970. 22 United Asia 28-34.

Shultz, Carl S. Federal population policy: a decade of change. 1970. 15 Vill. L. Rev. 788-800.

Simon, Julian L. The role of bonuses and persuasive propaganda in the reduction of birth rates. 1968. 16 Econ. Develop. & Cultural Change 404-11.

Singer, S. F. Is there an optimum level of population, AAAS symposium, Dec. 29-30, 1969. 166 Science 270-71.

Sirilla, George M. Government policy and family planning. 1966. 12 Catholic Law. 203-34.

Spengler, Joseph J.
Population pressure, housing and habitat. 1967. 32 Law & Contemp Prob. 191-208.
Population problem in search of a solution. 1969. 166 (3910) Science 1234-38.

Stycos, J. Mayone.
Opinions of Latin-American intellectuals on population problems and birth control. 1965. 360 Annals 11-26.
Politics and population control in Latin America. Oct. 1967. 20 World Pol. 66-82.
Public and private opinion on population and family planning. March 1970. 51 Stud. in Family Plan. 10-17.

Sulloway, Alvah W. The legal and political aspects of population control in the United States. 1960. 25 Law & Contemp. Prob. 593-613.

Tachi, Minoru and Okazaki, Yoichi. Economic planning and population growth. 1965. 3 Develop. Econ. 497-515.

Taeuber, Irene B. Population: dilemma of modernization in southwest Asia. 1964. 1 Asia 51-61.

Taylor, Carl E. Five stages in a practical population policy. Jan. 1969. 13 Poplt'n Rev. -37-44.

Tien, H. Yuan. National population problems and standardization of family size. 1970. 15 Vill. 801-07.

Tietze, Christopher.
Abortion on request: its consequences for population trends and public health. Aug. 1970. 2 Seminars in Psychiatry 375-81.
Modern methods of family planning. June 1967. 2 Advance in Fertility Control 13-15.

Turner, C. The implications of demographic change for nationalism and internationalism. Feb. 1965. 27 J. Pol. 87-108.

U.S. population growth and family planning: a review of the literature. Oct. 1970. 2 Family Plan. Perspectives (16p. supp. following p. 24)

United States: report of the President's committee on population and family planning. April 1969. 40 Stud. in Family Plan. 1-4.

Van Loon, Henry B. Population, space and human culture. 1960. 25 Law & Contemp. Prob. 397-405.

Ward, Richard J. Alternative means to control population growth. 1969. 27 (2) Rev. Soc. Econ. 121-38.

Weinberg, David. What state governments can do. 1970. 2 (2) Family Plan. Perspectives 30-34.

Winsborough, Halliman H. Social consequences of high population density. 1965. 30 Law & Contemp. Prob. 120-26.

Wishik, Samuel M.
A base line for evaluating national population control programs. 1969. 59 (8) Am. J. Pub. Health 1312-16.
The world population crisis; what it is and where to get information about it. 1968. 10 (4) Intercom 18-56.

Zaidan, George C. Population growth and economic development. March 1969. 6 Fin. Devel. 2-8; May 1969. 42 Stud. in Family Plan. 1-6.